T0050037

CHASING NORMAL

GROWING UP, LETTING GO, and FINDING JOY in BEING DIFFERENT

CRAIG GREIWE

Post Hill
PRESS

A POST HILL PRESS BOOK
ISBN: 978-1-63758-578-8
ISBN (eBook): 978-1-63758-579-5

Chasing Normal:
Growing Up, Letting Go, and Finding Joy in Being Different
© 2022 by Craig Greiwe
All Rights Reserved

Cover design by Cody Corcoran

Post Hill Press
New York • Nashville
posthillpress.com

Published in the United States of America
1 2 3 4 5 6 7 8 9 10

To those I have loved, for however long or short, and all that they have taught me. And to my parents, Rob and Kathy, who remain my safe harbor, every day of my life.

TABLE OF CONTENTS

PART I:
THE WAY DOWN

CHAPTER 1

COOKIES TO FREEDOM

have tried to forget nearly everything about growing up. That's what a lifetime of pain might do to you. Lately, however, I've realized it's only through that pain that I've discovered what it means to be authentic and real...and to have a chance at happiness. So, as I dig deep into my memory, it's funny the things I remember about my childhood, no matter how hard I tried to forget them. First, it's the church fairs that marked the passing of time in the monotonous routine of my tortured childhood. Church fairs are distinct and oddly important markers of the shifting seasons in rural Midwestern towns. There, time is not recorded by weather but by a ritual cycle of baptisms, graduations, potluck Christmas dinners, and for my hometown, Greensburg Indiana, a massive church fair. It's almost like Greensburg, and every place like it, is a less-cinematic version of the town in the movie *Groundhog Day*.

Rather than being tormented by living the same day over and over, the neighbors and families of my hometown find comfort in familiar daily routines. As long as nothing changes, everything stays the same. Which means that even if nothing's getting better, at least it's not getting worse. That's a Midwestern definition of optimism if ever there was one.

Even though for most there was solace in these communal rituals, for me, at nine years old, it was maddening. Every time the fair came around again, it was another reminder I could not escape my own personal hell. My life consisted of parents who would rather I were dead and a sister who came close to accomplishing just that several times. So once again, one warm October day in 1991, I was surrounded by shabby white tents and a crowd of people so large I had no idea where they could have come from, in a town that by all rights had not changed since 1953.

The gathering was a hodgepodge of folding tables and cheap, tacky stalls of homemade goods. One booth might contain hand-knit scarves from Louise, a forty-eight-year-old neighbor who perpetually seemed on the verge of a breakdown. Another stall, the "duck pond," was a game where children plucked small toy ducks out of a small plastic pool, revealing a colored dot on the underside, winning the child a sucker or a small plastic toy that would tragically be broken within four hours. But behind the cheap façades of these games and pre-Etsy stalls lay a huge business operation, raking in cash from hordes of people playing bingo and poker for hours on end while devouring overly sauced pulled pork sandwiches on white-bread buns served with a side of Ruffles potato chips, sold for $7.50.

Like all church fairs, there was always, of course, the bake sale. The women of Tri-Kappa had an extensive set-up, always located in a prime corner spot. The tables were heaped with brownies, cookies, breads, pies—anything these women of charity had baked themselves and priced to move. There was a "homey-ness" to these women, and it was always women, gossiping over whether Sally had made her fair share of lemon bars or if Mary deserved the limelight of being the first person whose offerings sold out.

I found myself standing at the baked goods table that one fateful day, miraculously holding a dollar bill I had unbe-lievably won. I had been wandering aimlessly, lost among the stalls and poker tables, when I saw a discarded winning lotto "scratcher" ticket lying in the dirt, accidentally thrown in a pile of losing tickets. The prize was a single dollar, but it would be my dollar. I snatched the ticket off the ground as if I had found the Holy Grail. Instinctively, I quickly looked around, worried its rightful owner might suddenly appear and wrest it from my grasp. No such claimant emerged, and I quietly made my way to redeem the ticket and then to the baked goods heaven. I stood alone in the sunlight, pondering my future.

I was a shy nine-year-old boy, anxiously clutching a sin-gle dollar bill in my hand. Dollar bills were hard to come by in my world, and when I could get one, it was more precious than a night where my father wasn't drunk. To say my family was poor would be grossly overstating our economic situa-tion. Dale, my father, had a garden—not as a hobby but to feed our family for most of the year because his primary job as a house painter didn't earn enough for us to live on. My mother, Joan, was a secretary and later a pre-school teacher. Neither was particularly lucrative and certainly not enough to raise four children, even in the poorest of small towns. There were times we foraged for food (asparagus grows abundantly in roadside ditches) or stole fish from the neighbor's pond.

So that dollar, firmly pressed in my hand, had not only economic value, but it also represented an opportunity I almost never saw: choice.

I could spend it on a raffle ticket and hope to win fifty dollars or more. But even by then, I had already experienced the crushing heartache and sense of hopelessness and futility after making that choice and losing the previous year. I could buy clothing, but even Louise's knit caps were four dollars, way outside my price range.

But I knew what I wanted. Working the fair earned my family free buffet meals for the day, but it did not come with dessert, and I desperately wanted dessert, like other people got. So, I stood there, in front of a table of baked goods sweltering in the sunlight under Saran wrap, dressed in threadbare cargo shorts, dirty shoes, and a sad green t-shirt. To me, it all looked like a selection of fine cheeses, tarts, and exotic pavlovas from the far corners of the world, things I would not even know existed until many years later. It's disconcerting when you learn much later in life how little you knew as a child, how sheltered your existence had been living in a dark corner of the world, surrounded on all sides by cornfields for years on end.

There I was, staring at the table of delicacies, and I chose the only thing I could afford. It was a flimsy white paper plate with eight snickerdoodle cookies. "$1" was written in black sharpie across the top of the plastic cover. I grabbed the plate and handed my money to a kind old lady, but she seemed puzzled by my choice.

"Don't you want something sweeter? Just a plate of plain snickerdoodle cookies? That's not *normal* for a child," she said in a drawl. I didn't care. I just wanted my cookies, normal or not. They were something I rarely had: something all mine.

It didn't matter these cookies were the only thing I could afford; I was proud. I bought the plate with my own money, and no one could take that away from me. When you are a poverty-stricken nine-year-old whose parents had to work the fair just for the free lunch, the sense of empowerment that comes with a single purchase can lift you for hours if you're able to divorce yourself from the reality that awaits in your train wreck of a home, a skill I had already deftly mastered.

I stared intently at my prize on the car ride back to our house. The afternoon was waning, but twilight had not yet set in. The plate was astonishingly thin, almost transparent, the kind that comes five hundred a pack at Wal-Mart. The Saran wrap was already coming off at the edges. But I thought if I focused hard enough on my prize, I could drown out the noise of my parents screaming at each other in another drunken fight. Suddenly, I realized why we were leaving, even though it was still light outside. My father had gotten so drunk dealing cards that they had asked him to leave; nevertheless, he was driving us home.

My mother had managed to acquire, under sympathetic stares from our neighbors, a tray of sloppy joes from the buffet table, which would feed our family for several days. All my father could manage to do was berate her for embarrassing him by accepting free food. My twin sister, Carla, sat next to me, blissfully staring out the window, which at the time seemed like an impossibly skilled response. I realized some years later it was a demonstration of her ability to focus on nothing but herself, even in the face of some pretty high-volume, vigorous cussing. I don't know where my two other siblings were, but they were much older, so they were long gone, off to state college or out with friends from high school.

As we pulled into our driveway fifteen minutes outside of town, a quarter mile from our nearest neighbor, I thought to myself, "That's okay, I have *my* cookies, and that's all I need right now." My tranquility did not last long. No sooner had we entered the house than my father's drunken rampage started up again. It didn't matter what day of the week it was or what was going on, Dale would find some target within visual range and zero in like a fighter pilot in the heat of battle. This would go on until he passed out snoring in a recliner after downing six or seven beers.

That day, he was ranting about how the church didn't appreciate all the things he did for them. He had painted the rectory, and they had paid him, but he donated the money back to the church. They refused to accept the donation, likely because they knew how poor we were, which was an attack on his manhood. His next complaint was that dinner was not ready, even though it wasn't dinnertime. Finally, he turned on his children, telling us how pathetic we were. According to him, by our age, he was already working and bringing in money to support his family. In his eyes, we were lazy, good-for-nothing, ungrateful pieces of shit who didn't appreciate all the things he had provided for us. In reality, his magnanimity consisted of a crumbling 1,000-square foot "house" that we crammed into, a fifteen-year-old television, threadbare blue carpet, worn linoleum floors, and a distinct lack of concern for our well-being. We didn't pick the corn from the garden fast enough. We didn't feed the dogs on time. To this day, I still wonder why a family that could not afford to feed itself also had two dogs, but that was just one of the many things that didn't make any sense to me.

My mother, of course, was no help during these tirades. After thirty years of marriage and fifty years of depression, she buried her feelings in secret stashes of ginormous tubs of ice cream from the Schwann's delivery service that came every other Tuesday. She would retreat to her bedroom, the only air-conditioned room in the house, to watch tapes of *The Young and the Restless* and *The Bold and the Beautiful*, worlds as far afield from our life as the ancient Romans were from space colonization.

Her bedroom door was always locked because there was no room in her escape pod for more than one person. Carla and I were left to fend for ourselves. We might have been fraternal twins, but there was certainly no bond between us. In the dog-eat-dog world that was my family, she had decided I would always be the lamb to slaughter. Perhaps it was self-preservation, or perhaps it was pure malice, but the result was the same: she escaped, and I bore the brunt of our parents' wanton abuse. As the only male around, I was also the receptacle for all of my father's guilt and regret about life, the young man who would carry on his name in disgrace no matter what I did. I would later learn his even more profound reasons for this dislike. At the time, however, all I knew was that I was a "pussy," "worthless," and a "piece of shit" who should have somehow, at the age of nine, figured out how to contribute more to our near-bankrupt position.

Whatever small joys I ever experienced—winning a toy instead of candy, finding a discarded scratcher ticket that had dropped a dollar on me as if from heaven—all vanished until Dale's sixth beer worked its magic and put him out. All I had left were my cookies, so I vowed I would take the only thing I had, those precious cookies, and I would leave.

It was time to run away.

While I would like to think I was somewhat brighter than the average child, I made several critical errors. For starters, I didn't pack a bag. While not an expert in running away, in retrospect, packing even some clothes would have been helpful. Second, I didn't take any money. I knew there was a few hundred dollars for emergencies hidden in in an old Folgers Coffee jar for the inevitable moment when the mortgage payment was even later than usual. That money would have been helpful, obviously. Third, and most importantly, I did not make a plan. I'm not exactly sure what kind of a plan a nine-year-old could have even come up with, but any plan would have been better than no plan. I had never been past the borders of our small town except to the nearby and only somewhat larger town of Columbus. Still, passion overcame logic. I just left.

And I took my cookies.

That's all. It was that simple. As the sun was setting, I just walked out the front door. I passed the thirty-foot-tall Douglas fir in the center of our roundabout driveway and headed straight for the gravel road that was the only connection to civilization. "Town" was at least eight miles away, although at that age, I'm not sure I knew really knew how long a mile even was. I turned left, passing our garden. The Garden, a horrible monster, a visual representation of just how poor we were and how lazy my father thought I would always be. I kept walking until I got to small grove of trees between our property and the neighbor's house a quarter mile away. I climbed a fence and sat down on the grass, my prized, thin white paper plate of cookies in hand, and I pondered my fate.

Reality hit pretty fast: this was a mistake.

I wanted to leave home; I really did. But I realized a few things: I had no place to go, no source of income, and my parents wouldn't care if I didn't come back, if they even noticed I was gone after a day or two. I didn't know which was more depressing. As I brushed back my dirty blond hair, I began to cry, tears pouring down my face and onto the cookies. I sat there for hours, late into the night, and just cried my heart out, begging God to save me. I begged for forgiveness. I begged for someone to love me. I begged for more than just cookies. I only stopped begging when I realized the only things that could hear me were the country birds and crickets whose calls I'd never understand.

So I ate my cookies.

One by one, I devoured the only part of my plan that existed. Slowly at first. I knew it was all I had, so I would need to ration them for a few days. Of course, when I realized eight cookies would not last a few hours, let alone a few days, I ate them all and crumpled up the plate in a fury I can still feel in my hands thirty years later. I pushed my tears back down, stood up, climbed the fence, and walked back home. To me, it was a prison I had been handed by fate. I was at least comforted by the knowledge that Dale would be passed out, my mother would be locked away in her room, and my sister, Carla, would be occupied by something that involved only herself.

I crawled into bed and imagined next year's fair and perhaps another plate of cookies. More than that, I imagined a world where next time I would keep going, walking to a life with parents who cared about me, to a life where I didn't scrounge for food from the ground, to a life where I felt loved, to a life that felt...normal.

I still didn't know what my plan would look like or how it might take shape; all I knew is that I had to get one. I was going to need it if I was ever going to leave this place, even if I didn't know what other places looked like.

Drying the last of my tears, I vowed to come up with a way out. My childhood strategy session was interrupted by the howls of my father, now awake from his slumber, screaming for the sloppy joes he had earlier rejected, and the sound of my mother unlocking her door to shuffle down the hallway to light the gas stove for him. That might be my routine today, I thought to myself, but now I had had a taste of cookies and the freedom they represented. I wanted more.

CHAPTER 2

IT DOESN'T GET BETTER

My early teen years were filled with childish dreams of running away, tear-filled nights staring at my bedroom ceiling, and prayers to God to save me, free me, reveal to me that this was all one grand mistake. By the time I was in middle school, I realized that God was not coming to save me. My Catholic guilt prevented me from seeing the solution myself, a fall off a steep cliff or an overdose or something else I didn't yet have the imagination for. During this time, a boy from town hanged himself, but I had no such courage. The only feelings inhabiting me were loneliness and loss. Loneliness because of my lack of normal human connections and loss—loss of I didn't really know what…perhaps the dream of a better life, like those I had read about in books.

In the absence of a willingness or capacity to take a knife to my wrists, I continued to suffer in silence. *The Prince and the Pauper* became both my most favorite and loathed book.

I used to lay in bed and stare into the void, fantasizing that I was a prince thrown into this impoverished state due to some mishap. I resented the fact the title character was rescued from his wretched state, while mine never changed. I built up resentment against the world and wondered why I had not been rescued from my suffering. Was it because I was different than everyone else? If so, if I could just glide through the world in disguise, could I, too, become a prince? Sadly, it was this impossible dream that sustained me with the slimmest of hopes.

Today, kids and teens have "It Gets Better," a well-known motto wrapped in stories of joy, entreaties of empathy from celebrities and everyday individuals alike. The campaign is an appeal to young gay kids considering suicide: give it time, give life a chance, and it will get better. For me, no such movement existed to extend a caring hand. My whole childhood experience had been filled not just with screaming and fighting at church fairs and at home but also with an endless parade of mental and physical torture from almost every person in my world.

My parents, Joan and Dale, continued to be at best indifferent and at worst completely malicious, subjecting anyone in their path to drunken abuse and insecure ravings. My older siblings were gone from the house and irrelevant, and my twin sister Carla was learning how to terrorize with the deftness of a pro. If I managed to get my hands on a toy, she wouldn't just take it; she'd destroy it. She once broke a Teenage Mutant Ninja Turtle in two just to prove she could hurt me with impunity. She would routinely pin me down and drive her long nails into my skin, drawing blood. The scars on my arms still bear witness to how effective and long-lasting her efforts were.

Then there was middle school, God's own special breed of torture for me. It was a world filled with predators like Carla. I don't know if they took their cue from her or vice versa, but every day was an exercise in endurance as everyone took a swing at me. Children seem to have the ability to sense fear and vulnerability. At the first sign of either, I became a target. Was it my fault? I *was* socially awkward. I was perpetually on the verge of tears. I had no friends. I received no advice from anyone except the mute stuffed animals in my room and the *Highlights for Kids Encyclopedia*, where, alas, there was nothing about being normal. I was the world's punching bag with no slogan to save me.

Instead, I spent my days running from class to class, trying to exit each one quickly and first to arrive to the next with the least amount of time in the hallways. Walk too slow, and my books ended up on the floor; even slower, and I could find myself shoved up against a locker with a vicious hand around my throat from someone who had nothing to lose and every desire to inflict pain and suffering. So, I spent my days darting back and forth like a sparrow, stopping only long enough to receive instruction in a cold plastic chair. The tinny ring of the bell marking the end of a school day was like an air raid siren, a signal to flee before the taunts and beatings came down on me like an avalanche.

If the gauntlet had been just a bunch of fellow teenagers in middle school, I might have escaped with minimal injury. But there was John Krowicz, the gym and health teacher who insisted on being called Coach K. He was the picture-perfect definition of a man who never really grew up, a Peter Pan. His position allowed him to avoid self-awareness and hard truths. He spent his days embedded with a cabal of thirteen-year-old boys, cracking jokes about abortion, penis size, and "faggots." That might land him in prison today, but in 1993, it made him the idol of children who didn't know any better.

For me, he was the monster-in-chief of my suffering, an all-powerful adult with a rabid fan base whose sole pleasure seemed to come at my expense, just like the boys who made him their king. I tried to remain out of his terrifying gaze but never seemed to get far enough away to escape his endless insults and public humiliations. Once, he had discovered my embarrassment about showering in public after gym class. He revealed this to the entire school during an assembly as a joke. He goaded and taunted me for being a sissy and a per-vert. Not content with a room full of laughter, when gym class ended the next Monday, he forced me to strip and shower in front of the entire class. Now, we might call that sexual abuse, but for me, it was just a normal cruel Monday. And so on to Tuesday I went.

Tuesdays turned into Wednesdays and seventh grade turned into eighth with no relief in sight. I can still see myself running up the stairs, hoping to make it to my next class unscathed. I can still see the fading, chipped white walls of the locker room as I cowered in the corner, waiting for the others to finish showering. I would then wash as quickly as possible, praying my towel and clothes would not be stolen. Still, even for a boy with no hope, who exists just to subsist, there eventually comes a breaking point.

One March afternoon, Krowicz was up to his usual antics during a basketball drill in class. It was an experiment in torture, like all the others of the past year, except that this one proved to be a bridge from my eternal sadness to righteous anger.

The students were split into groups and lined up to practice shots from the free throw line. After making a basket, they exited the line; if not, they were sent to the back to circle around and try again. The sole purpose of the exercise was to shine a spotlight on the weak. It worked, and our torturer descended on the last few students in line, myself included.

He watched as I failed, the ball wildly missing the net. Despite my future love of sports, Larry Bird I was not. Krowicz blew his whistle loudly, calling class to a halt. The last few balls hit the floor in the silent gymnasium and could be heard bouncing away ever so softly. Something about the thud of cheap basketballs echoing as they hit the hardwood floor of a cavernous gymnasium sweeps hope away with it. This sound was replaced with snorting by Mr. K, whose face was contorted in an odd mix of anger, pleasure, and anticipation. Krowicz knew he was about to inflict pain, and I knew it too. I was silently trembling in fear but also suddenly realized I had nothing to lose. How much more damage could he do? I had already been dragged naked through a locker room. He couldn't kill me; he would only keep me alive long enough to suffer, like a cat toying with a mouse, and I had repeatedly endured these games before.

"Do it again!" he screamed at me, throwing a ball hard and direct.

I didn't move a muscle and let the ball zoom past me.

"It's not my turn," I bluntly shot back. I had reached a crucial turning point, even if I didn't know it then. Words just fell out of my mouth without thinking. It was a spontaneous act of defiance emanating from the depths of my soul.

"I don't care! Do it again!" He blew his whistle and threw another ball. Even if I had wanted to catch it, it was aimed at my head, not my hands. I let it fly by me as I had with the first.

"No!" I said firmly, loudly, standing my ground. I was terrified, but I also felt something new: righteous anger and perhaps for the first time, even a tiny bit of self-respect.

If there was one thing this Peter Pan couldn't cope with, it was some "kid" challenging his authority. Nature had not bestowed intelligence, good looks, wealth, or happiness on John Krowicz. His only power was the traditional authority granted to adults over children, and now I was robbing him of that. My insubordination could not be tolerated. The class began to murmur ever louder.

Krowicz paused for a moment, staring at me, his pale white face becoming redder with fear, embarrassment, and anger. For nearly two years, I had taken his torture, bowed my head, and moved on. He had not been prepared for a challenge, however small.

He screamed at the top of his lungs and threw another ball as hard as he could. This time, I caught it, and without missing a beat, bounced it off of the floor just in front of him so hard he leapt to avoid being hit. With all the might and fury of his overweight frame and skin-tight, white polo shirt, he came lumbering towards me like an ogre. I fled, and he pursued. Nearly sixty classmates stood silently as a grown man chased a child, screaming and shouting at the top of his lungs. If you had paired this moving tableau with the soundtrack from a Laurel and Hardy film, perhaps it would have been funny. In real life, it was terrifying—a man twice my size blinded by rage could do bad things. It was insane and grotesque, a grown man chasing a child. This type of crazy was unfortunately standard in a small, impoverished school in rural Indiana.

I stopped running, and Krowicz finally caught up to me, gasping. He violently gripped my arm with the all the fury only an unjustly angry, small-minded adult could muster.

I could tell by the look on his face he'd never been in this position before. He was angry, sure, but also confused. As he stood looking at the dozens of kids around him, he must have realized suddenly how pitiful he looked chasing me. That scared him. His eyes darted back and forth, unsure of what to do next. He did not smile, he did not frown, and his expression was one of uncertainty. Students had rarely refused his instructions, and when they did, the power of his booming voice and the threat of detention were usually enough to restore order. For those who risked going further, in a pre-emptive strike, he got them out of the class before they challenged his authority. But from a weakling like me, someone who had cowered for years, this was a completely unexpected act of defiance. He was stunned, and it showed. It was only barely perceptible at the time, but my fear had ebbed away and was replaced by a sense, however small, of victory. I had moved this overbearing, cruel man from violent anger to utter confusion without really knowing how I had even done it.

He tried a new line of attack. "Run laps!" he commanded, handing down my punishment.

"No!" I screamed back, as I pushed what little advantage I had even further. He grabbed me physically tighter and threw me to the hardwood floor.

Now out of options, he shouted, "Go to the principal's office."

"Fine! I'll tell him exactly what you did! You can't hurt a student like that." I calmly answered. At that moment, the dynamic of power shifted. I had stood my ground and saw the emperor had no clothes. All that time, I had been afraid. All that time, I had allowed him to mock me, to embarrass me, to assault me, and he had done so simply because he could. In the years to come, this realization would serve me well. But then, in an instant, we both knew what would happen next. The first person to the principal's office was going to control the narrative. Would the story be one of the unruly student who committed the ultimate middle school sin of standing up to a teacher? Or would it be the overgrown bully who had physically abused a student after months of cruelty? The world stood still for both of us in that moment, neither of us knowing how this would end or who would be vindicated.

Mr. K. seemed to have realized the consequences before I had. Maybe a man whose future was hanging by a thread had some inkling of his true predicament. So before I could make a run for it, he held tightly to my arm and dragged me away. I had no idea what my classmates did when we left the gym; I imagine them sitting there by the dozens, idling until robotically responding to a bell and moving along to their next class.

Meanwhile, Krowicz marched me across the street from the gym facilities, through the metal and glass front doors of the school's main building, and straight to Principal Tom Toil's office. Krowicz ensured that not only would he arrive first to tell his story but that there would be no escape for me. He bellowed at me to sit down on the chair outside Principal Toil's office. I sat, now overconfident in my discovery of an adult's fear, combined with a belief that "right" would win out. I didn't really know how the world worked, but I thought that assaulting a student simply couldn't be okay. I knew that even in a small town where ignorance and poverty held sway, there must be some good, decent people. I felt safe in the knowledge that this principal, a man I had only seen at assemblies, would be like those admirable characters I read about in books I had buried myself in, a figure of justice and reason. At the time, I believed judges always had to be fair. But I was a lamb being led to the slaughter and completely blind to that fact.

The door closed behind the men. Krowicz began yelling about what I had done, and Tom Toil sat there listening. I could hear the principal trying to calm this lunatic down, trying to drag him back into some semblance of sanity. "Wait a minute," I remember thinking. "Why is the principal trying to calm Krowicz down? Why isn't he yelling back? Why is Tom so calm? A principal should not be coddling this abusive prick or providing him comfort. He should be upset and angry about what happened. A teacher had berated, abused, and beaten a student. This should be a principal's nightmare," or so I thought.

What I didn't know was that the worst thing in the world isn't anything at all…if it never sees the light of day. Only later would I realize that even though Krowicz hadn't seen the ramifications of his actions, Tom Toil had. He was going to take control the narrative to protect himself. This wasn't about some gym teacher; this could be a big problem for a middle school whose principal harbored greater ambitions. This was about self-preservation for Tom.

Precisely eleven minutes went by before Krowicz emerged. For me, every minute felt heavier, burdened by the weight of an unpleasant lesson: truth would not win out. Might was right. I was in for it. Krowicz did not even look at me as he left but marched on past and back into the bubble of his own little authoritarian universe.

"Greiwe!" Principal Toil bellowed in his angriest voice. "Get in here!"

I walked in and saw Tom's face was red, patches of rose poking through his pale skin. The realization of what was coming had not sunk into me. I was confused. Why would he be angry at me? I hadn't done anything wrong.

The situation became clear as Tom Toil ranted, raved, and lectured me for twenty-seven minutes. It felt like I was in a Dali painting, watching a warped and distorted clock mark the passing minutes by with no discernable effect. I felt like I had left my body. He would stop periodically to ask me a question, but they were all rhetorical. My murmured responses only confirmed his preexisting ideas. I wasn't just a disobedient student; I was a threat to this world. I had created chaos by questioning authority, and my wanton disrespect, for both himself as the ultimate authority and Krowicz, was a frontal assault on the middle school order of things.

In retrospect, now I realize Tom Toil was no idiot, and I oddly respect him for it. He did in fact realize the potential damage that a teacher physically abusing a student could cause. Rather than punish the teacher and reveal all of Krowicz's wild liabilities, such as drawing graphic chalk cartoons of abortions and cumshots on the blackboard during "health class" and parading students around the gymnasium for personal cruelty and amusement, Tom needed to contain the exposure and limit possible damage to his own career. Sitting in his office that day, I was just collateral damage. It wasn't personal.

I barely remember the rest of what Tom Toil said, except somehow the assault had been written out of the narrative, I was now the bad actor who needed correction, and expulsion was possible. What does an expelled student in a town with only one school do? It was a remarkable turn of events with no upside, another addition to my list of suffering. Later that day, others would stop me in the hall to ask me what happened. They said Tom's yelling was so loud and so angry that those who heard it stopped to listen and see if they could figure out what was creating such a commotion.

I was numb to the situation because I was a child without hope. I was traumatized because I had discovered there was no truth when you had no power. The adults in front of me had no real authority, but when challenged, lacking any other recourse, they simply changed the story. It was like watching a parent insisting you perform some task by counting down from the number "three" to enforce compliance. It's a game of chicken: will the child obey out of fear of impending punishment? Or will they realize the countdown isn't a threat—it's a sign of a lack of legitimate authority and really just a plea for some sort of negotiated peace? If a parent reaches "one" and the child still hasn't moved, will they simply start at three again but this time with a slap for added effect? Children with no power soon realize these tactics only have the power they allow parents to give them, time and again. Here I was, learning the mental gymnastics of parenting and failure at thirteen. I snapped back to reality as Tom Toil screamed at me.

"*Greiwe!* What do you have to say?"

Having been lazily staring into the distance and only slightly getting the gist of what my principal was accusing me of, I was adrift in thought. Somehow, I muttered something, but who knows what. Toil did not hear me.

"Speak up!" he yelled.

I took a breath and calmly stared at him. I had nothing to lose, and for the second time that day, fear drained from my body, leaving only an empty vessel shrouded in loneliness and logic.

"I don't think the school board is going to allow you to expel an A+ student with no record of any troublemaking," I said. "A teacher throwing me across the gym floor with sixty other students watching…. Someone will say something."

Tom picked up his phone inexplicably and then slammed it down as hard as he could. "How dare you…." he sneered. "How dare you threaten me!"

My casual indifference during the entire process had infuriated him, but now, sensing I had stumbled upon something actually dangerous, he moved beyond anger into something much different.

"I'm going to call your parents!" he roared, invoking that most ancient of threats to all children.

It took everything in me not to laugh. Yes, I was lost and even scared in this situation, but as one realization after another hit me and some amount of disassociation set in, so did my ability to live in terror and laugh at the same time. The man opposite me who thought he "knew it all" had tripped himself up and revealed his own stupidity. He had threatened to call the people who cared the least about what had happened or what the punishment was or wasn't.

"Great," I said in response. "Do you know the number? I'll dial. I'm sure you're going to love this." I knew the response he would get, but he was baffled at my pronouncement.

My flippancy was the final straw. Toil ripped the phone out and threw it across the room.

"Get out! Get out of here," he demanded. I sat blankly in front him, holding my gym bag, deeply confused by this new turn of events. What did get out of here even mean? Where was I supposed to go? Was I expelled? Who was going to fix the phone?

"I told you to get out!" he commanded. So, I did. I got up, left the office, closing the door behind me, and stood in the cavernous, empty hallway. Now what? My head was spinning. Was this all just some weird dream? Was there more to come? Was I supposed to go back to class? So, a teacher abuses you, a principal turns the truth inside out, and suddenly, here you are dropped into a sea of linoleum and concrete. What next?

Out of nowhere, the school's young "counselor" appeared. I knew who she was, even though we had never spoken. She was a mythical creature who flitted in and out of offices. I didn't know what counseling was or how it worked. She was a person with a title that might as well have been "forest nymph." In this case, her calming voice and soft approach indeed created an otherworldly air of assistance in the midst of my harsh reality.

"Why don't you come with me," she said kindly, beckoning me. Skeptical of anyone at this point, I hesitated.

"I think I can help," she urged. I followed as she guided me a few feet away into her office.

She told me she'd be right back and closed the door behind her as she left. I realize now she had just seen what Tom Toil was up to and had decided to intercept his ill-advised and angry march towards punishment. After she disappeared, there were audible murmurs in the distance through the thin wall. While I could not hear the words, the situation started to come into focus. Tom was telling this woman to get rid of me; she was trying to make him see the only path forward was by helping me. He relented after some time, perhaps realizing the futility of his own plan, and she returned.

"Now," she said, sighing. "Where do we begin?" She sat down in a chair across from me in what I supposed was her office. It was a quiet, dark, windowless room I had never seen before. Somehow the lack of windows provided some sense of escape and safety.

I don't know why, but I opened up in a huge outpouring of emotions, first about the gym, then about the tortures at school, then about my family. I am not exactly sure if this counselor knew what she was signing up for, rescuing me from a tyrannical, angry principal, but whatever she expected, she did not show any sign of hesitation or surprise. She would periodically get up and leave to reschedule an appointment that had otherwise been made but then return to our multi-hour session. For the first time in my life, I was telling someone my pain. I was unveiling a lifetime of grief. I was living it all over again but in the context of sharing, a concept I had never before experienced. I didn't know it then, but I was also saving my own life. All I did was talk, and that talk not only brokered a peace between me and Tom Toil, but it also built the tiniest détente between me and a world I hated.

After it was all over, I had missed the school bus and had to walk to my mother's job. She didn't ask where I had been or why I was there. She only stopped packing her purse long enough to berate me for making her late for her soap operas.

The next day, I went back to school, and no one said a word. It seemed, for a while, as if the whole school knew about what happened, and, rather than gossip, they simply left me alone. I guess if an event is really severe even middle school hellions steer clear. Teenagers' memories are short, though, so within a few days, I was once again scurrying from class to class like a field mouse being chased by ravenous cats.

Tom Toil never resurfaced in my middle school story. I would occasionally stop by the school counselor's office when it all seemed like too much to bear, but she would figure in my life only intermittently. I didn't yet know anything more was even an option. She seemed like an emergency brake, a resource to be used only when you're truly desperate. I wasn't aware adults came in helpful forms, too, forms who cared, forms who fostered compassion and kindness with routine engagement. There were two other outcomes. First, John Krowicz found other vulnerable targets and largely stayed clear of me moving forward. Second, I had a first glimpse of how the world worked.

I was not really old enough to comprehend how adults negotiated life with each other or how power dynamics were built and destroyed. I didn't understand what a scandal was and how to cover it up. I wasn't strong enough to leverage my own experiences for control or growth. But I had learned that confrontations had impact, however messy, so many more confrontations lay ahead. Real expulsion threats would come soon enough, as would more tears and bigger fears. But at that moment in middle school, I got a just a glimpse of the future, one where I played an active role in creating my world instead of simply subsisting in it. I had yet to learn know how to put my knowledge to use, so I still dreamt of running away and waited. Waited for freedom, freedom that would come with graduation, seemingly the only thing that could break the shackles of my nightmare in Greensburg.

CHAPTER 3

ABANDONED UNDERGROUND

The shackles of my life in Greensburg became tighter before they fell apart. Just a year after the gym episode in middle school, I found myself in even more dire straits, alone and abandoned, and for all intents and purposes, parentless as well as bereft of food, money, hope, and dignity.

My parents' abandonment didn't happen all at once. It was a slow-moving, painful ordeal that actually began before middle school. When I was ten, the local chapter of a charity gifted me the fees for a cheap summer camp two hours away from my home. I'm sure it was as a result of my good grades, general demeanor, and typical Midwestern civic duty, but to me, it was as unexpected as landing on the moon. I don't remember much of the week at the camp except that they insisted I swim in a pond (I refused), I learned to weave beaded belts (I became an expert), and I was befriended by a high school senior who was a camp counselor that took pity on my poor, lonely soul. My memory, however, is quite clear about what happened when I returned from this week in the forest.

When I got home, battered suitcase in hand and laden with woven belts and dirty clothes, I walked into the house and headed to my room. As I turned the corner of the hallway, Joan called out from the kitchen, but I didn't hear her. I kept walking, and when I got to my room, I saw a beautiful new desk and daybed. My parents had turned my bedroom into a hybrid office and guest room. I wondered who this new furniture was for. Why did my bedroom suddenly appear to be an office we didn't need with a bed for someone who didn't seem to be me? The next question was, of course, where had all my stuff gone? I didn't have much, but I did have my beloved stuffed animals to whom I poured out my emotions at night and half a wardrobe of tattered discount clothing. I went back out to the living room, suitcase in hand, and called to Joan in the kitchen just a few feet away.

"What happened to my bedroom?" I asked.

"Your room is downstairs now," she said offhandedly while chopping up some vegetable I can't remember. She motioned to the plywood door guarding the staircase down to our nearly windowless, unfinished basement. I stood there for a few moments, confused. The basement? Why would I move to the basement? However, in this house, I had learned not to question my parents' wonton cruelty, and I simply walked, trance-like, down the dark staircase. I now see just how far I must have fallen that I simply went downstairs without protest, without so much as demanding an explanation. I just...went.

As I reached the last step, I saw an empty room to my left with a concrete floor that had a cheap carpet glued to it with my old bed and wardrobe shoved into a corner. There was a shared closet that opened up between my new bedroom and a cobweb-filled storage room for the house. It wasn't totally dark. At least my new bedroom had a single half-window, below ground in a window-well, that allowed streaks of light to peek through for a few hours each day. I threw the suitcase down on my bed and sat there silently. I don't think I even cried. I just accepted that I had literally been banished to live under the stairs years before Harry Potter had made such a fate trendy.

I spent the next eight years before leaving for college in this cell-like apartment downstairs, scrounging for food, and going in and out through a set of concrete stairs at the back of the house. Up until now, I still told people I had my own apartment because I was far too embarrassed. Not because I lived in a hovel underground surrounded by the world's largest collection of spiders, homemade pickles, and a water heater. Not that I had to piss outside like an animal. I didn't admit it because I was embarrassed that I stayed even after my parents banished me to the basement and disowned me shortly afterward. Of course, being banished to the basement was not the ultimate punishment or last insult. Being abandoned was.

I don't know what motivated Dale and Joan to disown me a few years later when I was fourteen. To be honest, even now, I still can't fathom why. We were poor, and that wasn't helpful, but there are plenty of poor families filled with love. That wasn't ours, of course. My parents turned our suffering and their own insecurities and guilt into an unrelenting drumbeat of oppression that became a never-ending tsunami of misery, one that drowned our entire family. Whenever they could send a new wave our way, they did.

They also seemed to be filled with capricious malice, but being disowned was beyond even their normal level of attack. In general, the only time my parents usually bothered to yell at me was when they imagined I was interfering in their world, even if I hadn't. If a news bulletin interrupted Joan's ritualistically recorded soap operas, it was my fault. If my father, Dale, lost a house painting job because he showed up drunk, it was my fault. The reality was, of course, that none of it was my fault, but as they saw it, they bore no responsibility for their own failures. Although I had their attention in those moments and it drove me to tears in the dark corners of my basement room, their attention didn't stem from concern about me.

It was not the same as when other kids' parents yelled at them for coming home late or sneaking away to drink with friends. Those parents were *worried*; they *cared*. That's what others experienced, but I absolutely did not. My parents were just the right combination of damaged, poor, uneducated, self-centered, and a little bit evil. So, it wasn't just the poverty, I suppose, and I can't imagine they even cared enough to intentionally hurt me out of malice.

Their abuse also didn't come from the usual concerns about "drugs, sex, or religion." I didn't do drugs (in a million years I couldn't have afforded them), and sex was an afterthought when you're starving and struggling to survive. I even attended church every Sunday with a devotion matched only by an odd kid named Jesse, who became a priest.

So, out of all the possible excuses and explanations, I guess it was simply that they were sick, bad people, and I was a naive and immature teenager. Although I was an A+ student who never got into trouble, I somehow managed to fight with my parents any time the opportunity presented itself. Perhaps I resented them for the state of our family. Perhaps I resented them for the torture and suffering they foisted on to me. I definitely resented them for their selfishness and stupidity, and I made that known.

I was intelligent and well-read, while Joan was at the same level as her pre-school students and Dale was functionally illiterate. I have a distinct memory of him asking me how to spell "the." Of course, parents with bright children make do all the time, but Dale and Joan took special exception to my nonsensical insults borrowed from the 1978 *World Book Encyclopedia* that lived in my room. As a result, I took special care to fashion even more obscure insults, and they took special care to scream louder and longer. To say our relationship was simply fraught is like describing the 1906 San Francisco earthquake and fire as a tremor and a spark. So perhaps one day it was simply too much for them, and it didn't matter how much damage their decision to disown me would do.

The earthquake came first from my father. On New Year's Eve 1996, Dale had insisted we go to the "nice" restaurant one town over, and I refused. The soles of my only pair of shoes had actually fallen off, and I couldn't bear to go to what I saw as a "nice" restaurant with the soles of my shoes taped to my feet as I had embarrassingly done at school.

My father was drunk, which goes without saying as far as any day of the week during my childhood was concerned, and insisted we leave. He called me a pussy and a faggot, even though he had no inkling then I was gay, and neither did I. He just screamed random insults at me until finally, he simply blurted out that I was not his son.

At the time, I thought he meant I was not the son he wanted, surely true, or the son he needed, also true. But what I would come to learn a decade later was that he had accidentally revealed I was not actually his biological son. Had I known right then that he was infertile and that they had resorted to donor eggs and sperm, it would have oddly made those moments of insults easier to bear, but I didn't know that then. Instead, I was left with the searing reality that as he walked out the door, he no longer considered me his son.

I was hit with the sudden realization that I was being disowned that New Year's Eve; my refusal to go to the restaurant in taped-up shoes was the straw that broke the camel's back. The family left without me that night, while I buried my tears in a threadbare brown puppet kangaroo. No self-respecting fourteen-year-old should ever have to use a stuffed animal as an emotional support mechanism.

Lest I think that what had happened was just another drunken fight, however, Dale pulled me aside the next day, perhaps to start the year fresh with clarity amid his hangover. We went outside into the frigid cold and sat on the back step, with him calmly encouraging me to sit. In a Hallmark movie, this would be a tearful apology. My life was the cruel inverse.

"Last night…" he began as his voice trailed off.

I said nothing.

"I don't know who you are," he said. "You're not like me. You're different. You just make everything so hard."

This was not the direction I thought an apology would go. Ironically, it was also the most eloquent I had ever seen him.

"I don't know what you want from me," I said pleadingly.

"Nothin," he shook his head. "I don't need nothing from you. And you don't need nothing from me. You're on your own."

At the moment, I didn't comprehend the depth of what he was saying. He then just got up and went inside, leaving me sitting out in the cold. To me, it seemed just a weird moment in a series of tragic parenting mishaps. To him, it meant much more. The only difference I would notice in the coming weeks was that Dale kept an unusual distance, and there was far less yelling, and there were far fewer insults.

Clarity came from another direction, however, a few months later. It was during Easter, and we had just come home from an extended family gathering. Joan retreated to her room, as was her wont, while the rest of us scattered to the wind. No matter Christ had risen, Joan was seeing to her own salvation first.

She was the type of person who put Girl Scout cookies in the freezer for herself, and when I was naïve enough to eat one as a child, she berated me for stealing "her food." She was concerned about herself above all else, and her children were there to simply serve her various needs. Our inability to do so, along with an unwillingness to shower unconditional love on a woman who never had love, led her to her job as a preschool teacher. Three-year-olds will attach themselves to anyone in sight, and she strategically placed herself between the Fisher Price toys and apple slices to that very end. The only thing separating her from true martyrdom was her inability to actually crucify herself, except verbally.

As the day wore on that Easter, Joan remained isolated in her room. I wandered up from the damp basement and knocked on gently her door. It was past dinner time, and I was hungry. I heard her shuffle across the room, open the lock, and return to bed. I eased open the cheap hollow door and closed it behind me. Her soap opera blared from the TV.

I sat on the floor for a few moments, watching the show with her. Then she sighed heavily, her only acknowledgment of my presence so far.

"Will there be any dinner?" I asked her.

She pushed "pause" on the remote.

"Why do you keep interrupting?" she shot back at me, as if I had been asking questions for hours. Her chest rose with the weight of her entire obese frame.

I didn't know what to say. She kept the television show on pause.

"My whole life," she began, "I was never good enough for anyone. And I thought when I had kids of my own, finally, I would have something that loved me. But it's never good enough for you."

Sadly, Joan's rationale for having children and understanding of proper parenting practices were less than accurate and showed no awareness whatsoever of what the word "parent" could even mean. I sat there, quiet.

"You know, it's one thing for your father. He's done with you," she said.

"What do you mean, done?" I wondered, squeezing my eyes in confusion. Yes, he had been distant, but I had welcomed the reprieve from his yelling and fits.

"You're no son of his anymore," she said. Suddenly, the New Year's conversation with Dale flashed through my head with a whole new meaning.

"I can see why," she continued. "You're just impossible. I thought you might be a little like me—you're a bookworm too." She relished her *Reader's Digest*; I relished the encyclopedia.

"But you always think you're just better than us. Nothing's ever good enough for you. Nothing's ever enough for you. You're supposed to be here to love me, and instead, you're just a burden."

I sat in silence. Joan was oddly calm for someone who was cutting her own child from her life. Her eyes began to well up in tears at her own misfortune.

"I just don't know why God would punish me with you. All I ever wanted was children who loved me. And I got you. I just can't do it anymore."

I don't remember the rest of the conversation, except she made it clear that I was on my own, and my twin sister Carla would not suffer a similar fate. Carla, for her vindictiveness and evil nature, was at least somehow more "normal" to them, like the child they expected. My aspirations for what I read in books had made me want something more, and wanting something more made me realize how little we had, which in turn had brought me to my current crisis. Joan explained that she and Dale would no longer be providing for me in any way. Anything I needed, I had to get for myself. If I was hungry, I'd need to find my own food. I'd need to get a job, even though I wasn't legally allowed to work.

From time to time, they might bestow on me some act of benevolence: a ride to school, a dollar, or a plate from their dinner, but I was to expect nothing. Of course, I still had a roof over my head. The basement cost them nothing, and I was out of sight and so out of mind. I continued to attend extended "family" gatherings when called upon for appearances' sake and to avoid the prying eyes of the authorities. Even then, they had a semblance of understanding that what they were doing was wrong and needed to be hidden. I was so crushed and hollowed out, I didn't protest and went along. But little by little, I would find myself on the receiving end of less and less from these people. Some years later, Joan went as far as to hand me a piece of yellow legal-sized paper with an itemized list of costs she had incurred for my upkeep, a bill asking for reimbursement.

From that Easter 1996 on, they became *the* mother and *the* father, or Dale and Joan, or even "the originals" since "the biologicals" turned out to be belatedly inaccurate, but no mind. They would never again be *my* parents, *my* siblings, or *my* family, if they ever had been. This distinction still confuses people, but eventually, they figure it out. People who behave so awfully do not deserve the generosity or the emotional tether of possessive adjectives.

So yeah, I tell people I was disowned by my parents, which is true, and got my own apartment, which is close enough. I could not admit to being stupid enough, damaged enough, and simply desperate enough to stick around and piss outside during high school because I wasn't allowed access to the bathroom upstairs. Who would remain in a home after being disowned and forced to fend for himself? I mean, technically, it was my apartment but only in the sense no one else wanted to live down there. Had I known then what I do now, I would have scrawled on the walls, "What the fuck is wrong with you people?" in my own blood. I would have to include myself in that condemnation, but back then, I just thought it was par for the course. I cried every day at school without revealing the truth to anyone—not that I had anyone to actually confide in. I simply accepted I did not belong upstairs with Dale, Joan, Carla, and the non-existent guests who never came to the room that used to be mine. I did not matter to the family that raised me. I was truly on my own.

Freedom did not come until the end of high school. But that seemed like something that was light years away from my present reality. In fact, the future and my possible freedom felt further away by the day. As I approached high school, I found myself on a precarious cliff on the edge of existence. I was bankrupt, poor, hungry, and alone. Abandoned. I had been cut loose and left to fend for myself. I had been deprived of even the few resources my impoverished parents had provided.

By the age of fourteen, both of them had disowned me, leaving me to blindly navigate the world with only the survival skills of a child. They had never cared to teach me much of anything except those things painfully learned from their abuse. And while the situation was abominable, I was so beaten down, I didn't even think it could be different.

All of this would be one thing if it was just an emotional journey, but for me, it became a physical one too. Suddenly, I wasn't just the crying kid in the forest or the teenager tossed around a middle school gym; I was truly alone. Emotionally. Physically. Financially. And it was all just so matter of fact. Perhaps that's how life is. Sometimes, it's captured in vivid memories of childhood experiences or principals yelling at you. Other times, the most traumatic of moments become mere bas-reliefs in your story. That's how it was when I was banished and abandoned underground.

Then, of course, there were the practical decisions that followed. My parents' lack of any material or emotional support forced me to make virtually impossible decisions just to survive. First, I had to get a job, and the options in our podunk town were limited to food service or clothing retail. After evaluating the situation with the gravity it deserved because my entire life depended on it, I made a strategic decision. I reasoned I would be able to scrounge up food; the parents usually put out leftovers, even if mostly for the dogs, but clothing cost money and was expensive. An employee discount would be more valuable. I talked my way into a job at the only high-end teenage clothing store in town and then worked my way up the management food chain to greater responsibilities and greater discounts.

When a new department store opened in town and I knew it would put the place where I worked out of business, I quickly leapt from the doomed store to the new mega-store. At the new job, I worked every hour I could get, hustling my way over after school and then driving myself home after midnight in a 1980s tan Chevrolet Nova that miraculously still ran. It was a lucky $900 castoff from Carla; the parents had bought her a car, and she said it was too ugly and too cheap for her tastes. Simply because the car was already paid for, it cost them nothing to toss me the keys and consider it done. They then bought my sister a nearly new brown sportscar, which she promptly totaled. They bought her a second. I still don't know where they found the money for such an extravagant purchase…twice. The whys and wherefores of the situation didn't matter much anyway. I was trapped in my own hell, below ground, alone. It would stay that way, as I lay there every night, staring out my half window, wondering when the first ray of hope might shine through. It did just a few years later as the end of my high school career approached.

CHAPTER 4

RED BOOTS

I s it too obvious to say that Hell can feel like an eternity?
Weeks turned into months, and months turned into years.
The only view I had was not of an exit from my monotonous misery but of weeds in the window well of my basement
bedroom. School was still no better.

The only respite came at work, of all places. I worked at
the most expensive clothing store in town, which was not
saying much. What I didn't admit to myself at the time was
that the long, tedious, endless hours at work were a relief
amidst the chaos of my life. I was surrounded by nice things
I could never afford. I thought, "Who has the money to just
buy candles and let them sit at home?" or "How many colors
of the same sweater could one person need?" It didn't matter
that these were mid-market home goods or cheap imitation
cashmere. To me, these products put me adjacent to world I

wanted to be part of, at least when within the four walls of "Goody's Department Store."

The reality of my life didn't even contain fake cashmere. Every day, I returned to re-reading *The Prince and the Pauper*, rivers of tears, and a lot of scurrying through hallways. My life was like some sort of horrible treadmill, and I was waiting desperately for a rescue that could never come soon enough. The bullying continued, and the independence of graduation seemed light years away. My painful home life was unrelenting, and the idea that someone might ever love me seemed impossible. It was like I was playing a memory game to match hidden cards, but every card you turned over was the same. As I got a little older, there were unexpectedly occasional flashes of hope. Just getting closer to graduating from high school seemed like light at the end of my long dark tunnel. And sometimes a star peeked out through the dark clouds of my life. One bright spot came to me when I least expected it in the form of Ruth Cash, my high school French teacher.

Mrs. Cash was a shining beacon from a world beyond the yellow press board walls that encased my everyday life at Greensburg High School. I was invited, as part of a class, to an afternoon gathering at her house. I was overwhelmed by the spotless floors, vaulted ceilings, and artisanal decor. I had only seen things like this in magazines I tried not to read because they made me even more depressed about the dilapidated shack I called "home."

She came from another universe, a cosmopolitan one of fluent French and Chinese, luxury goods named Chanel or Hermes, and recipes from exotic cookbooks. Things so far away from my life in Greensburg I barely knew they existed. Even if I had been fortunate enough escape my basement dungeon, the nicest thing my family owned still would have burst into flames in Mrs. Cash's world. The appeal was about more than material objects and foreign verbs themselves; it was what they signified to me. This woman exuded confidence, sophistication, and composure. She knew all the important books, she sat on State Boards and advised Governors, and ran the French club like the concurrently prestigious and hostile clique that it was.

It didn't matter what rumors about her circulated, most conjured up from the malignant boredom of life in a small town. She must have had heard them, in a town so starved for gossip that people ended up fabricating it, but she brushed it off, held her head high, and did not deign to address anyone she thought didn't merit it. If Miranda Priestly's character from the movie *The Devil Wears Prada* had doppelgänger who taught high school French and English in someplace like Greensburg, it was Ruth Cash. How she ended up there was a mystery. It was as if she were trapped in our godforsaken town by some weird curse for offending the gods in her youth.

She let everyone know exactly how she felt about such a posting, far beneath what she deserved. As a result, Mrs. Cash was politely distant, never too friendly, and always on the boundary of interest and disinterest. She was also incredibly tough in class. She was my French teacher for four years, as well as the teacher in charge of my senior advanced English class. She never hid her disappointment in mediocrity or a lack of effort, and she never broke the wall between teacher and student, lest I or anyone else think she was more friend than simply "only as friendly as manners required."

Even when I had tried my hardest, if I fell short of the mark, I could expect a searing critique. I can still remember turning in an essay on *King Lear* and getting it back with a short note: "Incoherent and nonsensical. I don't even know where to begin. Start over." A girl named Angie, the closest thing I had to a friend, though never too close, became indignant at Mrs. Cash's treatment. Angie pointed out that Mrs. Cash never made comments like that on other people's papers. She didn't understand why this woman was so harsh on me. But Angie saw only part of the picture and consequently didn't understand how I saw the situation. I dared not reveal how I really felt. It was complimentary in my world to receive so much attention from someone. If Mrs. Cash were indeed angry at me, at least it was because she cared about what I did, or so I thought. That was a feeling I had not had from anyone before, and it had a profound effect.

The only time I was ever noticed by my parents, who had long since disowned me, was when they thought I was interfering with something in their world, even if I wasn't. I seemed to have existed only as an outlet for my parents' anger. If Mrs. Cash was the closest I'd get to an adult caring about me, I'd take it, even if she routinely embarrassed me in front of my classmates in an effort to push me to be better.

"Read aloud," she said one day, so I did.

I read from a book we were studying, "Just then, everything went awry, and she wondered where to turn next."

"Stop!" Mrs. Cash yelled, leaping from her desk in the corner of the room with a spark of joy that excited her for some unknown reason. The entire class grew silent. We all knew this could go south very quickly.

"Say that word again," she commanded.

"Which word?" I asked.

"Just read the sentence again," she insisted.

So again, I said aloud, "Just then everything went awry."

"There! Spell it." She wrote in big, chalk letters as I spoke aloud. A. W. R. Y. "Pronounce it!" she said with glee. I said it again, finally hearing the source of her amusement. I had been wildly mispronouncing it, *aw-ry*, as in *aww-reee*. Why? Because no one had ever told me it was "Ah-Rye." How was I to know? These were things that parents, relatives, friends, mentors, or other adults who might have cared would have taught me, but I had none of that. As with most things, I had taught myself how to read and what to do in even the most basic situations; I tried to learn by mimicking others. I had done a pretty damn good job of it, excelling at school with a high grade-point average and hopeful for some kind of college scholarship. I had been planning to leave Greensburg since I had finished those cookies that dark night eight years earlier and had struggled, studied, and clawed my way toward a future that included some kind of opportunity.

Every step of the way, I made mistakes, almost derailing my journey because I lacked someone to teach me how to plan or behave properly, but I always raced to correct my mistakes and caught them almost every single time—*almost*.

Then there were moments that went "awry," where I was exposed. I had just made a mistake, and Mrs. Cash had caught it before I could correct myself, move on, or cover it up. I had made a monumental error in front of her and the class. *Awry*, a word that would haunt me. But somehow, her behavior wasn't malicious, even if it hurt. Which made it just a little bit better.

"I don't know why she does it to you. She doesn't do it to anyone else," Angie muttered again, walking away after class. Her compassion was endearing, and it almost gave me the feeling that I had someone to talk to, though I didn't and couldn't. Angie's empathy, like my parents, served her own purpose and anger and had nothing to do with me and everything to do with her own feelings about Mrs. Cash. In the meantime, I knew there was something more going on with my teacher—something heartfelt, not cruel. I would, many years later, be vindicated in those feelings.

I had always felt she pointed out my mistakes and tried to keep me rooted because she cared, but I had grossly underestimated how much. Many years later, we went to lunch, and we started talking about class and her treatment of me. To me, it was like decoding a secret message for the first time. For Ruth, her behavior was just ordinary. She explained it was "so simple," as Miranda Priestly would have said. She saw a student who was overly confident in his ability to deliver, to memorize, and to play a role. I was playing a role, after all, trying to be someone anyone would care about, even if I didn't know it at the time. In her mind, however, she thought I was mistakenly trying to become a clone of the most generic sort, someone perfectly average and bland. She worried I would become a "Stepford" man, obsessed with chasing what I thought I was supposed to be like but never discovering who I really was. So, she had taken every opportunity not just to help me pronounce words but to do it in a way that shook me into honesty, in the hope I would realize there was more to life than being like everyone else.

So simple, she had said, but only to her. Sometimes I wonder if she had known my whole story if she would have acted differently. I was not prideful as she had thought, I was terrified. I was not arrogant; I was nervous. I was not boastful; I was deflecting. I was not nearly as smart as people thought I was, but if being smart was the only way out, and that's all I had, then so be it. If the world found out I was a fake and an impostor, I might have been trapped in Greensburg forever, an inverted sort of Dorian Gray, someone cursed to live eternity in mind-numbing misery while his better half thrived on a canvas.

Even though Mrs. Cash made every effort to hinder my Stepford journey with harsh truths, not knowing what I already faced, it's not as if she made things worse. If her demonstrations of caring left me half miserable and half meaningful, it was still more than I got from anyone else. So, in my senior year, I waited for an opportunity to bring a smile to her face as a sign of my profound gratitude for even the possibility of mattering to her. That sign would be a pair of red cowboy boots.

Red cowboy boots were certainly not a common item in Greensburg. Wanting them might seem an odd impulse. But in the topsy-turvy world of high school, it would mean a great deal to the person who meant the most to me. I got the idea one day when Mrs. Cash was reading, as she often did, from a children's book as part of her lecture. She was always incorporating themes from these sorts of books into the larger life lessons she imparted to us in-between literary criticism and grammar.

Turning to a page from *The Little Old Lady Who Named Things*, Mrs. Cash described the main character's footwear with excitement. Mrs. Cash explained that this little old lady, with no children and no family, who named things, had the most fabulous red cowboy boots. She was completely thrilled at the idea of this old lady enjoying life in ridiculous, absurd, red cowboy boots. I don't exactly remember what lesson we were to get from that lovely children's book. What I do remember very clearly was the look on her face as she showed us an illustration of the boots. It was at that moment I decided to get her those shoes.

Red cowboy boots were not cheap. I realized this endeavor would take some effort. First, I managed to get a credit card without my parents' knowledge. I used it to pay the nearly $200 for Sheplers to ship me a pair in eight to ten weeks. Figuring out Mrs. Cash's shoe size for this non-refundable gift was an entirely separate adventure. It involved several embarrassing favors and requests from people I would not really label as friends but who, for whatever reason, pitied me enough to help. My plan was coming together, even if I'd have to miss two debate tournaments to work extra to get enough to pay for the boots.

Then the shoes finally arrived. I had been anxiously tracking their progress for weeks. I was beside myself. I had even saved up money to buy red wrapping paper and researched how to wrap presents so they didn't have to be ripped open. (You wrap both pieces of the box separately and then hold it together with ribbon and bow.) I did not know I was gay then, but there were indications, like exhaustively researching gift wrapping techniques for just the right look.

Perhaps I also wanted to show her I could inhabit her rarified, elegant world.

The day the boots were ready, the school bus arrived on schedule, six o'clock in the morning. I lived in the rural countryside, so school bus routes were epic. I was the first pickup and then had to endure a ninety-minute, suspense-filled trek that was always on the verge of being turned into a gauntlet. Every moment on the bus required defensive and offensive tactics: trying to prevent people from sitting next to you, warding off unwanted questions and attacks; avoiding newcomers; and somehow, on this day, keeping someone from ripping apart my present. Much like my search for Mrs. Cash's shoe size, it was as if the universe somehow knew this moment mattered more than anything else to me and for once accommodated my prayers.

However, even arriving at school did not end the dangers. The bus dropped us off at the usual time, but because some students arrived as much as sixty minutes before the start of the school day and had to be monitored, administrators had decided to house everyone in the cafeteria until school started. Shoving hundreds of teenagers into a single room in the early hours of the morning involved a risk of torture even for the middling, average kids. For me, such injury was all but a certainty. Years before, I learned this and had created a safe space for myself, which I now used with my precious red cargo in hand.

As a freshman, I had joined the "Academic Team," a kind of sports team for trivia quizzes and coached by the school librarian. I worked my way into getting a key to the library for "extra practice." I used that key for three years, sitting on the hard, carpeted floor of the darkened library before school started, far away from the madhouse of the cafeteria. For hours on end, I would cry, study, write, read, and do anything to avoid being noticed by the teenage terrorists just down the hallway. Nestled between book stacks, I was alone, and that meant peace, if just for a few minutes every morning before the school bell shattered my alternate reality.

On that day, the stacks provided more than a personal refuge; they were a safe haven for my precious cargo and the staging area for the final part of my quest. I waited where there was a direct view of Mrs. Cash's classroom. I nervously checked her door every few minutes waiting for her to arrive. Finally, she came down the hallway, hustled into her room, and closed the door. My heart sank—she usually dropped off her bag and did a few quick errands, which would have given me an opportunity to slip in and deliver the gift unnoticed. I was not only terrified of life in general, but I was also painfully shy, and giving Mrs. Cash these boots was the biggest social risk of my life. For all I knew, she would take the box and hurl it at my head as an egregious overstepping of boundaries without even opening it. I held my breath, praying to a God I still believed in, despite everything that had happened to me. Finally, she left for her usual mail run. Waiting until she rounded the corner, I raced to her room, deposited the box gently on her desk with a tiny card, and ran out. I was not particularly poetic, so I made it simple: "*I know you always wanted a pair. I hope these fit. Craig.*"

I retreated to the library to await the start of the school day, as well as every class break and "passing period," five minutes of hell as seven hundred students shuffled from one end of the building to another. Waiting for English class that day, navigating the five minutes of student-inflicted tripping, taunting, and abuse between classes, study hall, physics, and AP Chemistry, seemed like an eternity.

After an anxious blur of getting through the morning, the moment of truth finally arrived. My classmates and I wandered into English class, all thirty-four of us. Mrs. Cash began the lesson as she had many times before. The class, her behavior, all the students…everything was exactly the same as before the pivotal moment when I placed that magical box on her desk. There were books to discuss, assignments to hand out, and critiques to be done. I began to panic slightly in my chair. I began to wonder, "Did she not get the box? Did someone take it?" I looked around, but it was not visible, if it was even there at all. Had she hated the gift? Did she even open it? How could I have been so stupid as to think that I, an impertinent high school senior, could give a gift that meant something to someone so far outside my world? After all, her comment about the red boots had been months ago, a lifetime away, and even though her face had revealed a secret yearning at the time, perhaps it had passed. I was miserable sitting there. I had reached for the stars and fallen short, barely even noticed, if at all. I thought "Why bother trying at all if this is how it turns out?"

Just before class ended, Mrs. Cash handed back papers, as mine hit the desk, something slid out. It was a sealed envelope made from a kind of fancy paper I had never seen. I did not dare open it during class. I had no idea what it might say, and every day in a world where you were an isolated, lonely alien, discarded, disowned, and impoverished, made for a fragile, difficult day. The tiniest thing could send me running out of class in tears to the safe haven of the library stacks. In retrospect, the powers that be at Greensburg High School should have known something was up since I routinely disappeared from class in tears. But if they did, no one ever said anything, much less helped with my struggles for shelter, food, and basic love. I tucked the note away and searched Mrs. Cash's face to try and make eye contact. Would there be any indication what she was thinking? No, she was too poised for that.

The bell rang and as the students raced to their next class, I spent my five minutes deliberately. I stepped just inside the library doors, straight past the front desk and into the back office for some privacy. As I set down my books, my heart was pounding. I gingerly opened the envelope, being careful not to rip its precious paper. The bells rang for the next class, but I didn't care. I couldn't move. I stood there, scrutinizing every line of Mrs. Cash's exquisite cursive handwriting. It read:

> *Craig,*
>
> *I cannot tell you how grateful I am for the boots. Not just because I have always wanted a pair, but because you did something people hardly ever do. You listened. And you used what you heard to bring me joy.*
>
> *Thank you,*
> *Ruth Cash*

Holy hell!

I sat, stunned. For the first time in my life, I felt what it was to bring joy to someone and to experience gratitude in return. In eighteen years, most of it fraught with distress, mistrust, and emotional isolation, as far as I knew I had never brought joy to anyone. No one had ever said thank you for anything. I was breathless. Not because I was in love, or I had a crush, or idolized Mrs. Cash but because I mattered to someone, if only just a little, and I felt it inside. I was caught up in a moment where, at long last, something I had done mattered to someone else. I had never been so thankful for a simple note, and there have only been a few times since when I have been so moved by someone's words.

High school would be over in a few months, and I'd be on my way to a new life and a new chance at being normal and just like everyone else. Mrs. Cash's efforts to dissuade me from my Stepford journey had not taken hold. There could and should have been someone to teach me a few things that might have saved me a world of pain in the future, but there wasn't. The plain plate of cookies taught me to hope and plan, abusive gym teachers taught me authority was vulnerable, my parents taught me people would make me disposable if I didn't make myself invaluable. Mrs. Cash was the one who imparted something positive: she gave me the knowledge that I could matter. I could make a difference. I could *be something* to someone. That was the only lesson I really learned in high school, and I would make the most of it in the years to come.

CHAPTER 5

KEVIN AND JOE

In August of 2000, my long hoped for and meticulously planned freedom arrived. Even if I didn't have any idea what life after high school was like, I was willing to take a chance on pretty much anything. Desperation breeds risk, and I was desperate for a world and a life that was like everyone else's—*normal*. After graduation, I left everything I knew behind, miserable as it was, and fled into the night in a rickety tan Chevrolet Nova. The car was crammed with my meager belongings as I drove three hours to my personal Oz: DePauw University, the self-styled "Harvard of the Midwest." I had found some balm in the occasional kindness of others growing up, but I thought my true salvation lay in this bricked-faced and gilded promised land.

Not that I could afford college on my own, but I had been blessed through luck. In the waning days of high school, I had amassed five-hundred-dollar scholarships through essays and competitions, but it was still not enough to bankroll my big jailbreak. DePauw cost over fifty thousand dollars a year, an astronomical sum almost impossible for me to imagine. At the last minute, however, two separate foundations awarded me full scholarships. Ironically, it wasn't really me or my future accomplishments they wanted to fund; it was my hard-knock story that tugged heart (and purse) strings. As I would discover, the occasional upside to my deep poverty was that well-heeled schools, filled with the children of the wealthy, sprinkle cash on a few lucky people from the other side of the tracks to feel better about themselves. DePauw would not be the last place where I was able to leverage this moral whitewashing. If the negligence and brutality of my youth had somehow created enough cosmic goodwill for this sort of payoff, so be it. I wasn't going to argue about this one. At least this made me feel that all my suffering was not totally in vain.

DePauw, a school of 2,200 students, was a universe away from everything I had ever known. For starters, it was stunningly beautiful, absent the signs of poverty I had thought the norm. It was like a different planet. Every building evinced the university's signature Georgian architecture, and brick walks lined with leafy green trees bound them together. Even the landscaping evoked a quiet sense of staid superiority, the result of expensive and deliberate efforts to ensure that whoever entered campus palpably felt the University and its inhabitants' entitlement and privilege to the bone. DePauw was not just a "good school," it was also one of the most expensive in its category and wanted you to know it. I had never experienced such a rarified atmosphere, and I fell in love with the school because of it. What else would a child of poverty and abandonment, who knows no better, do except embrace shallow, shiny affluence?

Strolling through DePauw's campus, admiring East College, the impressive 150-year-old building at its heart, I believed my life had finally turned a corner. Maybe it was going to be okay. I had somehow slipped through a secret gateway to a future with…*hope*. This was my chance to be like everyone else, people whose lives were not filled with years of emotional trauma, people who were not worried about where their next meal was coming from. Perhaps, I thought, I could be just a normal college student. Someone free to explore the beautiful eccentricities of Soviet Politics or the literary nuances of *Anna Karenina*. This was my chance to break free, my moment "to shine," to "grow," and to "explore." I had not just memorized the admissions brochure but embraced it as a credo. I would do it all at DePauw, a place that gave me a sense of privilege and strength that some grew up with, but which was entirely new for me.

Reality quickly set in, and it stuck me in the face like a polar blast. Honestly, I had no idea what it even meant to "shine," to "grow," or to "explore." Everyone else seemed to have actually benefited from their lives before college. They seemed to have had childhoods like those in the storybooks I had idolized. They had been free from the crushing desperation of having to find food. While I had been folding sweaters for pennies, my fellow students' elementary and high school years were used to discover their passions and interests. They seemed to be fully formed human beings; they knew the ins and outs of university life and how to extract the most from every moment. They knew how to "rush the Greek system" and get into the sorority or fraternity of their choice. They knew what sports they were good at, while I could not even hit a ball. They knew what the right weights were to use at the gym. They knew how to behave in class and analyze a Jane Austen novel and which clubs to join. But most importantly, they had an easy time befriending one another, something at which I was woefully inexperienced. Having to meet new people in any situation was excruciating because of my complete lack of life experience and social skills.

Fate can sometimes hand you a foil to counter your own failures. At the beginning of the fall semester of my freshman year, I met a gregarious student named Cody. He was strikingly pretty, even if a bit thin and pale. His jet-black hair was expertly tousled, and he was incredibly outgoing with everyone. The noise level rose three notches when he entered the room, and his laugh carried across the dining hall. He was awe-inspiring to me.

College was also an escape for Cody; he had left the straightness of his youth behind and embraced his homosexuality with zeal. This was vividly on display as he regaled us with stories of his latest conquests: Zach from the football team or Tim from the swim team or Michael from the lacrosse team. It seemed he had a penchant for finding "heteroflexible" athletes and falling in love with them all in a single day. I envied his freedom, but I would not have even known what to do with it if I had it.

I did not know I was gay, even if others might have had an inkling. When you're busy foraging food and plotting an escape from Devil's Island, dating and sex get put away somewhere. That somewhere was deeply buried inside me, and I had never experienced attraction any more than one would a small gust of wind as it brushed across your face. My time had been fixated on simply existing, not living, not that same-sex attraction would have gone over well in Greensburg anyway. Cody was the first gay man I had met, one of the first people I knew who lived the opportunities that filled every moment to their fullest. For him, every day was a chance to embrace joy. One could hear it in his voice.

One day, he approached me as I sat eating lunch with Brady, a female classmate of mine. They knew each other from theater classes.

"So whooooo are youuuu, darling?" he asked, leaning in across the table. "We haven't met!" His unvarnished, genuine enthusiasm for life and the ease with which he occupied his own skin was electric and terrifying.

"Craig," I said. I could not have been more unremarkable in tone or appearance compared to his suave approach.

"Yes, but whoooo are you? What do you do? What drives you? What are your passions? Who do you love?" he elaborated with a curled smile reminiscent of the Cheshire Cat. He raised an eyebrow on the last phrase, clearly asking if I was also gay. These were the sort of uncomfortable and probing questions I always feared and avoided at any cost but were simple, normal conversation starters to Cody.

"I, uh...I..." I struggled to respond.

Brady jumped to my defense. "Cody, be nice, and leave him alone!"

"Fine, darling! I'll see *you* later to run lines," he said, bounding off as quickly as he had arrived, like a midsummer thunderstorm.

Social interactions like that with anyone were uncomfortable for me. Socializing was terrifying and left me baffled. How should I answer their questions? While other students wanted to get to know each other, I didn't want anyone to get to know who I was, or at least who I was before. I wanted a clean break from the past and to not even talk about it.

I had grown up with my face in a book or behind a cash register, with three-minute conversations limited to cliches over a counter amid the beeping of a price scanner. These other students at DePauw had grown up socializing: watching MTV, hanging out at each other's houses, talking about music, crushes, NFL teams, and *Dawson's Creek.*

I did not know a thing about these pop culture mainstays, so my conversations were limited to the knowledge I had memorized from the 1978 *World Book Encyclopedia* or to our schoolwork, behavior that gave me a reputation as a bookworm and know-it-all—not a great social label in college. I hadn't developed any social skills and lacked even rudimentary conversational skills. Now that I was in this world, I saw I needed to make some serious changes. The only way I thought to do that was to watch how others behaved and mimic them, while hiding my ignorance, lest I be exposed as an imposter. I was trying to build a house while also living in it, always a dangerous situation.

As I had before in high school, I tried to copy those around me to learn what I didn't know, which was almost everything, but I fell woefully short early on. There was simply too much to learn, and it was all happening so fast. The new world of possibilities was already caving in around me, and time was running out. It seemed as if somehow, magically, others simply knew which group they fit into and which friends they would make and hold on to. I failed again and again in these interactions, always leaving a trail of awkward behavior like breadcrumbs that led back to the secret horror of my childhood. Cody was just one example. There was also Lisa, Casey, Shelby and Gavin. If I had just opened up and been honest, maybe it would have been different. But I couldn't take the risk. Vulnerability breeds honesty and connection, I know now. But eighteen-year-old Craig had no such insight or self-awareness to develop it. Instead, I made stammering responses and had a fear of social settings that terrifyingly stalked my life in the first weeks of freshman term.

Still, in the face of all my difficulties, I persisted. I began to perfect the art of learning while doing, a big game of pretend while concurrently figuring out how the whole damn thing worked. I was only partly aware of what I was doing; it was just an instinctive act of desperation. In the midst of this gargantuan experiment, trying to make up for eighteen years in just a few months, I was saved by my only and first-ever friends: Kevin, Brady, and Mandy, who also served as my role models.

Kevin, Brady, and Mandy were also part of the Honor Scholar program at DePauw, an academic elevation program. They included me in their clique out of a combination of compassion and gender balance. Mandy and Brady, the girls of the group, had become close friends quickly, and Kevin had decided on day one he was in love with Brady, which made an unbalanced triangle. I was added to the mix to keep him company and away from Brady, at least until she broke up with her high school boyfriend and succumbed to Kevin's charms. How could she not? He was the classic All-American boy: dark hair, olive-toned skin, bright eyes, a square jaw set with earnestness and genuine kindness. As we navigated our freshman fall, the differences in the upbringing between Kevin's world and mine were a case study of opposites, although I was the only one aware of the differences.

Kevin, like me, was also a bit out of step but in a completely different way. While I was awkward out of inexperience and painfully shy, he was friendly and outgoing but overly excitable, a characteristic that endeared him to everyone. He was the stereotypical nice guy who was always there, a center of attention without an ego. I was just trying to blend in behind the curtains. My story was the stuff of Dickensian drama; he had grown up in a Norman Rockwellesque household with two parents, two kids, and a summer house on Lake Wawasee. His parents had even bought him a new blue Jetta for college, and he was obsessed with becoming a writer. Such a career path confounded me; becoming a writer was not something one did where I grew up.

It was a huge risk, I thought. What happened if you didn't succeed and you couldn't make money? I was on a mission at college. I knew that if I didn't quickly figure out a career for when the four-year reprieve of college ended, I would land back at home or in the nearest city, drifting through a purposeless life as clueless and opportunity-less as I had been before. Not so with Kevin. He was on a mission of exploration.

I needed college to be a clean break and a way into the world other people inhabited—the world of Mrs. Cash, the world I saw in reality shows when I got my first television. Kevin already lived that world. I could not take risks like thinking about becoming a writer because my choices were driven by the likelihood of success. The combination of fear and purpose became a strong undercurrent in my personality that would only reveal itself in my late thirties. It was as if I were a dark, smoky, sharp whiskey. Kevin had no such quandaries or concerns, and so "writer" it was, his choices in life reflecting a personality that resembled the bubbly and enthusiastic effervescence of a freshly popped bottle of champagne. Everyone likes champagne, while dark whiskey has an intense taste that is carefully acquired and rarely partaken of. I felt lucky Kevin took to any drink, including me.

He also had a passionate commitment to social engagement, something I became interested in when no other guides presented themselves. Kevin had been in all kinds of clubs and teams in high school and did the same at DePauw. I wasn't really sure what a social life really meant, so I just tried to follow his example. I admired him; I liked him. Other people liked him, and I wanted them to like me too. So, I was determined to do as he did—that was how I was going to get anywhere near where he was in life.

He did theatre, so I did. He joined the cheerleading squad, so I did. Yet as much as I succeeded, I was still failing. He "rushed" the Greek system, and so did I. He got into a popular house, a ticket to success at a place where most students are in fraternities and sororities. The only fraternity that offered me a place had just re-started and offered entry to anyone and everyone. Even my rudimentary knowledge of social life at college told me to say no thanks to that social poison.

The contrasts between us were also reflected in our classes. He chose political science classes and thrived on philosophic thinking. I chose the same classes, but I couldn't understand why people spent so much energy thinking and not more doing. I struggled in French and worried endlessly about everything; he glided with ease. His obstacles seemed minor and inconsequential. "It'll all work out" seemed to be his unwritten motto, while mine was "Fix it or die trying."

Outside of class, I had tried to teach myself to be a college student like the other 2,200 people around me. I quietly observed and did the things James, Matt, Kelly, Kate, Brandon, and so many others did so effortlessly. Of course, I was so focused on learning what they did I never took a moment to see what I was doing or who I was becoming, an imitation of a person instead of my own self. This was made strikingly clear one spring day by a professor who did not fit into the helpful and compassionate category: Joe Heithaus. It was strangely fitting that he was Kevin's favorite professor but also the man who tortured me.

Professor Heithaus, who insisted being called Joe, had a rehearsed informality that made me uncomfortable. He taught a class on literature and philosophy during the interwar period in our Honor Scholars' program. A tall man with wild hair, Joe was the type of professor who relished late night debates about nothingness and had a willingness to question everything. Kevin's intellectualism, his inclination to leap first and look later, a fearlessness born of a stable childhood, had made him Joe's favorite student.

There, I did not follow in Kevin's footsteps. By this point in my college career, my efforts at mimicry had produced someone who appeared confident and thoughtful. In reality, I was hesitant and anxious, a byproduct of my desire to minimize the opportunity for mistakes and public excoriation. The result was being over-prepared for every class and social situation. I was exhausted, lonely, and struggling, but I never told a soul. Every day was simply a stress-filled death march. I might escape being unmasked, or I might take one step too far and face ridicule, embarrassment, and exposure. This meant I doubled down on every effort to be perfect. As a result, I was diligent and aggressive in my studies and determined to get the most out of each moment of class. I was Joe's worst nightmare.

Whereas Mrs. Cash had wanted to help me, Joe treated me as an enemy. He shot down and ridiculed my every question. He was hostile to any idea I had that ran counter to his. He embarrassingly mused in front of the class about why I was so small-minded and unwilling to engage in what he believed to be essential academic dialogue but what I considered unproductive rambling.

Kevin and I had a long talk about class late one night, where he urged me see things from Joe's perspective. It occurred to me that I could turn the discussion in to a paper, thus showing Joe I was willing to engage in the process he wanted…and drawing on his favorite student couldn't hurt. I did this in a unique way for an assignment, copying our texts into an essay I submitted. I never stood a chance. I got it back with a giant "F" written as large as the top of the page would allow.

Nevertheless, I was learning that diligence and determination can be a bulwark against attack, no matter how earnest. When Joe sought to tear me down, I doubled my efforts. I continued to do well academically in spite of his attempts to ensure grades that could damage my chances for success after DePauw. He had his philosophy; I had my fear. The latter ended up being stronger in the end, and I got a decent grade, but not before a confrontation with Joe at the end of the semester.

It was during one of Joe's mandatory "writing conferences," where he explained why you received the grade you did on a major writing assignment. Ostensibly a moment to learn and grow, Joe used them to reinforce his influence over his students' lives, an opportunity for him to prop up his image as a man of the people, a professor who cared. While that may have been others' experiences, it was not mine.

"Craig," he began as we sat in his office, "I really take pride in being a good guy. I *am* a good guy." It seemed like a poor start if what was to come required this initial caveat. Good people don't start conversations by insisting they are good people.

He continued, "When I grade my students' papers, I root for them. I overlook the little mistakes, the missing commas and misspellings. I want to see them *learning*. In class, I hear them out when they're wrong about underlying facts and try to guide them gently. They need to be cultivated, fostered, and encouraged."

These were all inspiring sentiments but not my experience with him. This was going somewhere soon enough, but I really didn't know where, so I just sat there.

He continued, "But with you, it's the opposite. I root against you. When I am grading a paper of yours, I look for every mistake. I relish every opportunity to mark you down, to catch every fault, to give you a worse grade than you deserve." I may have only been a freshman, but I knew that this was one of the most inappropriate conversations one could ever have with a teacher. Krowicz may have twisted my arm and thrown me to the ground. Joe was trying to break me mentally.

"And for the longest time," he said, "I just didn't get it. I didn't understand *why* I wanted you to fail so much. At first, it was because I thought you were so closed off to new ideas. Every time we discussed Nietzsche or Kant, you simply refused to believe in them. You attacked every idea. You scrutinized it, you looked for the fault instead of the underlying message. But this," he slapped down the paper I had turned in, "made me realize I had it all wrong. How could someone who was refusing to intellectually engage in ideas turn in something so goddamn good? And then I realized: I was wrong. And I want to apologize to you. I was wrong."

I was struggling to find words. What response should I give? "Thank you?" "Okay?" He had admitted to brutalizing me for a semester and then being wrong. Now what? But I didn't have to say anything. Joe kept talking.

"What I realized about you, Craig, is that all your questions and your attacks...it's not that you're not open to new ideas. It's you testing them. You beat them up, you subject them to the greatest scrutiny, and only then, once you've decided an idea has been tested enough and validated, you reach out and *snatch it ever so quickly* while no one notices, make it part of your life, and then pretend like it's always been there. You're doing it all the time, Craig. I see you, now. You're literally just hiding who you are and what you really think from everyone."

Joe may have only been talking in the intellectual realm, but I felt that I had been read within an inch of my life. I didn't know it then, but he was right. All my efforts that freshman year had been exactly what he described, even if unconsciously. Instead of being who I "was and what I really think," as he had exhorted, I had spent my time consumed with hiding and mimicking. Those efforts had come to define me.

"Craig, you will get an A in this class. But I'm asking you, I'm begging you, to stop being so closed off. You need to explore. You need to open up to others. You need to find out who you are and be free."

I said nothing. I didn't know if he could see the emotions hiding behind my expressionless face, but we both knew, as correct as he might have been, what he suggested was never going to happen. I was in too deep and too far. Even with the world of possibilities I had at DePauw, I was crippled by a fear I had not yet come to recognize. It's often said your past follows you; what is not said is what that will look like. I had scrupulously studied others' behavior, trying to act like them, creating a new person to escape my past. I was chasing normal, but I had not become normal.

Fear kept me from blindly leaping forward. Instead, it sent me down a path that left me isolated, quietly suffering on my own. I was still dashing in and out of the dining hall when it opened so I wouldn't be seen eating alone. I kept up the appearance of thriving around Kevin, Brady, and Mandy, but when they were not around, I was crying tears of loneliness. I was living on a constant shuffle between "pause" and "play." When I was on my own, I had no idea who I was, and I had no real sense of self. I stood on the verge of a new future, seeing new possibilities and hope for the first time, yet I was unwittingly undermining what little progress I made.

No matter how hard I tried, it would all come crashing down around me in an ill-fated, righteous, and principled struggle. A crisis at the end of my sophomore year brought me to lows that I had never dreamed possible but also handed me a second chance to start over. Sitting with Joe, I didn't know this at the time. All I knew was I was angry at him and so many others. I was angry at the parents, angry at my fellow high school students, angry at the lady at bake sale, angry at anyone who had a part in making me into *this*, a person of only last resort. I grabbed my paper and retreated to the leafy green of the East College lawn. For the time being, I still had a life to lead. Even if it was not truly my own, I *needed* it. This place, this practiced effort. I needed something, anything to keep me from slipping backwards. I needed normal, or so I thought, and I'd do anything to get it.

CHAPTER 6

THE ATTACK

A year after Joe's brutal takedown of my failed attempt to craft a life that filled the hollow feeling inside me, things took a brutal and unexpected turn. In August of 2002, I found myself on the outskirts of Los Angeles. There I was, laying on a garish comforter at a Ramada Inn on Vermont Avenue, two thousand miles from everything I'd ever known. I had a sense as to how I had landed there, but it was complicated, and I couldn't really put it all together even though I had all the facts. I was in a daze, as if intoxicated, and everything was mixed up.

To give an example of just how discombobulated I was, I had actually done the unthinkable: I asked Joan to drive with me to Los Angeles. I suppose her presence was simply practical; I didn't know how to drive across the country, and monster or not, she did. One is truly out of options if relying on the goodwill of a woman (a stranger, really) who had disowned you six years before. Of course, Joan was oddly happy to join because it made her feel wanted and needed, the two things she desired most in life. I was once again serving a purpose, but it had nothing to do with me.

The trauma of the events at DePauw had so emotionally crippled me that I let someone who had excommunicated me from my family ride along for the trip across country...to start over in a city I had never visited at a school I had never seen, the University of Southern California. My leafy Midwestern existence was being exchanged for something unknown, and unlike leaving Greensburg, leaving DePauw was a punishment, not an escape. I had ended up in California due to one key mistake: I mistakenly thought I could matter to people and had tried to procure a gift to prove to them just that, but unlike Mrs. Cash's boots, it did not go well. In my desperate attempt to feel useful again, I made some very bad and impulsive choices, ones that didn't lead to a cheerful thank you note. This time it led to a hostile university administration and the loss of almost all that I had thought I earned. How did I end up in California with Joan by my side?

A year before, it had been different. I had built a life at DePauw; Joe Heithaus be damned. I had earned my stripes, as it were, remained friends with Kevin, Brady, and Mandy, and tried to make other friends. They didn't call me, but at least they picked up the phone when I called them. I had been active in the theater program, and people had, shockingly to me, actually come to shows I had directed. What I had wasn't perfect, but it seemed like things were getting better, perhaps because I was so far from what I imagined was the rock bottom I had come from.

There were still many nights I lay in bed weeping, wondering if I'd ever find love and hope. What college student hasn't? I was still sneaking in and out of the dining hall so as not to be seen eating alone, but every so often, I found someone to eat with. Baby steps. I was holding on and making a go of things. I took it as some sort of a sign when my dorm burned down but my room was somehow spared. I, too, could rise from the ashes. Even if I was poorer than everyone I knew in friends, love, money, and opportunity, it was the most I had ever had. Standards are low when you start at zero.

I had thrown myself into school. I earned honors in every class. I befriended professors and had dinner at their houses. I had become part of a university system that rewarded merit and obsessive diligence with special access. I used that access to glean information for stories in the school newspaper written from perspectives not known by others at the University. I didn't want to be a journalist, but it made me feel special, even if in a small way. Students wondered how I knew scholarships were being cut or which professors were getting hired. Every article I wrote was like a pair of red cowboy boots. People spoke about the articles, to me and to each other. I even won the award for best general news reporting from the Society of Professional Journalists for a series I led and wrote.

If I hadn't let my guard down, I might have continued to make progress. But instead of keeping a clear head and remaining careful, I started to believe the bullshit, the false praise from the faculty who granted me access and made me feel special. Mandy, Kevin, and Brady didn't need me as much, but these mentors, these professors, Ralph, Pam, Marcia, and Stephen, still did. Young and impressionable, I wrote article after article reflecting their priorities, passions, and feelings as if they were my own. I thought I could be of value to them. I would *matter*. They were like a new Ruth Cash. I didn't realize they had manipulated me. In my quest to fill the emptiness from a lack of a sense of self, I lost what little identity I had developed in college. It would not be the last time, but it certainly was the costliest. It took only one wrong move, one "protest" article, written to please my parental stand-ins.

The thing about college is that even the smallest event can take on monumental proportions, particularly inside the confines of a small, leafy green liberal arts school. Some of the practical realities of the outside world didn't make it through the campus gate. On any given day, one could find a dozen students fervently protesting for the rights of migrant workers or grey-spotted squirrels. Ten years later, burdened by the routines of work, family, and trying to make ends meet, some of them might not even remember making signs and marching. But at that moment, a moment of youthful idealism, ask one of them how they felt and it would elicit a passionate speech explaining in extraordinary detail the squirrel's plight at the hands of loggers. My deep attachment to professors who made me feel special meant their own protests became mine; I wore their opinions as if they were bespoke suits for me with disastrous results.

It all started with a simple provocation, a rumor, albeit a true one. I heard from Professor X that Professor Y was on a hiring committee that had been instructed to hire a minority candidate, something I would later discover was illegal. A third professor supposedly had proof that teaching credentials had been forged in a different hiring process. In the world of academia, where integrity and independence are highly prized, such revelations were seen as an attack on values more than any concern about their legality. Diversity is important, even essential, but my mentors had never heard of this type of malfeasance at a university of this caliber, one as important and special to them as DePauw. These professors had internalized the institution's hubris and artifice, and I had drunk from the same poisoned chalice wantonly and irresponsibly.

Those same mentors encouraged me to speak to their sources with a whispered urgency, intimating the fate of the university was one the line. "You must talk to them," they said, and I did. The result was a remarkable piece of meticulous and accurate reporting. My time had been taken up with dozens of interviews revealing a careful portrait of a university so hellbent on increasing the ranks of its minority professors (a noble cause) that it had skirted (and yes, possibly broken) the law. The topic was so hot the school newspaper, theoretically independently owned and run, a bastion unto itself, refused to publish the article. Finally, under pressure of my threat to go public, they buried the story in the last issue of the fall semester of my sophomore year.

My professorial mentors were impressed, honored, and kind. They said I was doing them and the University a service in exposing this scandal. I felt like I mattered again. I was thrilled to be valued, a useful servant to the cause of those who seemingly cared about me. Little did I know I was a pawn in a bigger game, one that would burn down the house I had built, much like my dorm that semester. The insolated nature of university life affects not only the students but also, I would soon learn, professors and administrators. I had unintentionally become the opening salvo of a world war inside DePauw's little bubble. Unrealistic idealism or not, what I would have given for just a little protest then, even a small one. But no such luck.

Initially, it seemed as if my article had gone strangely unnoticed. All was quiet on the Western front. The normal atmosphere of final exam madness smothered the campus, with students darting between buildings, trying to keep warm in the frigid winds. What little time they had, they all spent dreaming of the coming holiday break with their families while basking by warm fireplaces in their fraternity houses. Students were unconcerned with almost anything that didn't affect their parties, studies, or grades. I imagine that will never change. But my life, like a grenade with the pin removed, was going to explode, and when it happened, the damage was swift and significant, enough for students to put down their drinks and grab their pitchforks.

Out of my sight and unbeknownst to me, dozens of professors attacked me at emergency faculty meetings with vitriol usually reserved for comic book villains. Soon, students I didn't know were actually spitting at my feet as if I had done something to them personally. I was told if I took certain classes, I'd be given an "F" to show me the "value of grade diversity." I was called a racist, a baffling claim; others came to my defense and called for the heads of the University's senior administration. There were rumors that I had made it on to the agenda of a meeting of the Board of Trustees, the rough equivalent of an ant targeted by a howitzer. No student should ever be a topic of discussion in the "Winter Retreat," filled with a of bunch of people who'd rather toast the growth of the endowment than deal with the real task of running a good school. Unfortunately, I became the headline. I was the news instead of a reporter. Students and faculty were swarming menacingly. That winter, whatever progress I had made constructing my own life started slipping away.

When the talk about lawsuits and legal defense funds began as I returned from winter break, to say I was floored doesn't even come close. Everything I had was on the line and perilously close to vanishing. I was empty, numb, and lost. I became a zombie drifting between classes, unable to pay attention to an opportunity cost curve or Soviet Leader Yuri Andropov's political machinations. This was not how my sophomore year was supposed to go. I begged Kevin, Brady, and Mandy for help when I could get them to listen. But they just looked at me sympathetically, the way one might look at someone dying of a fatal disease—you know it's bad, but you can never know what it really feels like.

We were all just nineteen years old; our biggest concerns were supposed to be term papers and worksheets. I was hand delivered a single-spaced, seven-page letter from the provost threatening expulsion because of the article. He admitted the facts were all true but simply too controversial. I didn't know how lawsuits worked, but I was being told to get ready for a lot of them. The University was all-powerful, they warned me, and would use that power as much as they could. The whole thing was made even worse because the state judicial bench was composed of many DePauw alumni.

I was on the verge of losing everything I had fought for, however little it was. Kevin, Brady, and Mandy had gone their separate ways into the increasingly cold winter. I'd hear from them only a few more times that semester; no one wants to be around the walking dead.

My solitary lunches became more frequent; what few burgeoning friendships I had fizzled out. Even my caring professors, who became consumed with the ballooning controversy I had started, left me unprotected. I came to know the embarrassing and traumatizing ritual of an *ad hoc* university judicial committee. The adjudicator, unfortunately for the scales of justice and me, was of course a member of the administration itself. The fox guarding—or worse, owning— not just the henhouse but the damn farm. I could viscerally feel the walls closing in around me.

To be completely candid, lying on those awful sheets in California months later, I realized exactly what had happened after the fact, even if I hadn't seen it coming. It may have felt like a bad trip at the time, but the mental toxins still coursing through my body were the product of a series of my bad decisions. These destructive choices were a result of chasing anything that seemed to give me worth. I now realize if you don't know who you are, you might become a person you don't actually like very much.

When those wrong decisions pile up and you're confronted with losing your whole life, you will take whatever life raft is offered, even if it means giving up everything. Desperation—that is how I ended up in California, I realized...that and one final shove from my endearing alma mater.

At the end of my sophomore year, as the crisis crested, I was summoned to the office of the head of financial aid. She led me into a cavernous office of pink tufted chairs and dark pillows. I knew where this was headed: DePauw had complete power over my fate in the form of dollars and cents, the scholarships that kept me in school. What need would there be to expel me when you could just cut off my money? I was here because of their money; now the piper had to be paid.

I don't remember her name, but I vividly recall her light, almost joyful, tone.

"So, I was talking with the university president yesterday," she began, sacredly invoking the man whose legacy I was threatening to tarnish. "And we both agree that it would be very healthy if you spent some time away from campus."

And there it was. The ultimatum: leave.

"I don't know what that means," I insisted.

Her tone softened. "Well, we took a look at your credits, and it turns out that you're so far ahead, you could take an entire year off and still graduate on time."

Now I was really confused.

"I can't do that," I stammered. "I don't know what I'd do. How would I live?"

"Well," she continued with a well-rehearsed serenity, "it also turns out there are some opportunities available to you if you'd be willing to take a year off. President Bottoms and I both think it would benefit you and the University to take some space, and we think we've found a way to help, provided you will follow our advice."

The alarms went off in my head. This was it. This was the moment, but a completely different moment than I had anticipated. Somehow, I was not being expelled. My scholarship money was not being cut off. I was being thrown out, to be sure, but tossed out into the street with an ever-so-subtle bribe of a miniature golden parachute. President Bottoms was a gentile Southerner at heart and perhaps mindful of the small chance my expulsion would give his opponents something to use against him. Removing me from the equation would instead allow him to outflank them. I was a pawn that he could easily sacrifice, better to spend the money in a tactical move against his real opponents. I was nothing.

"When I reviewed your financial records," she continued, "it turned out there was an excess of scholarship money. Enough for you to live an entire year off campus, studying wherever you want to, doing whatever you want."

I sat there, speechless.

She continued, armed with her superior hand. "I know you've been accepted into the semester-long arts program in New York, and they have room in their housing there for you for a full year. And I'm told USC will take you as a visiting student too." I had, by pure chance, applied to USC with Mandy when she briefly considered transferring, even though at the time I had no intention of going.

"Okay," I said.

I was numb and in shock; I had no idea how to process what this woman was telling me. I was being handed a gift of a year in New York or Los Angeles, but at what cost to me?

Some might jump at the opportunity, but these cities might as well have been on Mars. It was clear I would never be allowed to return to DePauw; she insisted I had enough credits that a junior year away would lead to an early graduation. I was losing what little I had and being exiled to a faraway land where I didn't know anyone and would have to start all over. A land where I was starting in a cheap motel on top of a comforter that belonged in the trash with a woman I couldn't stand.

As Joan, the "mother," snored in the bed next to mine that night in Los Angeles, I stared blankly at the ceiling, blithely unaware what the future held. I'd reinvent myself again artificially. I would come within spitting distance of success at my new school, only to flame out again, this time in a spiral that would lead me to failure, assault, and suicidal ideation. At some time in the future, I would finally be ready to maybe, just maybe, stop for one damn second to figure out how life really worked, instead of acting as if I did. But this wasn't that moment.

Instead, I simply resigned myself to starting over again and hoping not to fuck it up this time. It was early in the morning before my grand entrance into a legendary university I had never heard of a few months earlier, ironically founded by DePauw graduates. I realized I was further from Greensburg than ever before, and the stakes were higher. If I failed this time, if I did not build a life, or worse, if I built one but destroyed it again, I would likely not get a third chance. I could not go back to DePauw, and I did not want to go to Greensburg. There was no other way forward. The pressure was crushing, like someone grabbing the inside of my chest and twisting. I'd realize, years later, this visceral experience was my first panic attack. Back then, I had never even heard of such a thing. I had known only loss and fear...and resolve, however tenuous. This was my chance. I'd try again to be what people wanted. I'd try again to glean from others how to behave, learning while doing. However, this time I'd be armed with the knowledge of how things went wrong the first time. I could do better, I thought. Time would prove me wrong. The future would not go as hoped or planned, and in fact, I would end up to falling from even greater heights than before.

CHAPTER 7

A FIRST KISS

B y the spring of my first year at USC, which served as my junior year in college, it felt as if I had finally fallen into a rhythm again, even in this unfamiliar land. College, it seemed, was not particularly different no matter where you went. USC was founded by DePauw graduates a century earlier, so it felt similar to its verdant predecessor in the Midwest, even if the faces were different. USC students had a more pronounced sense of privilege and were generally wealthier, but they seemed to want the same things as students in Indiana. In this new little bubble, which I rarely left, even to visit greater Los Angeles, the only things that were clearly different were a distinctly better climate and that I was starting over again. I still ate solitary lunches, buried myself in classwork to avoid thinking about my life, and longed for authentic human connection. The opportunity unexpectedly came knocking that first spring at USC. It happened outside the bathroom, of all places, in my new fraternity, Kappa Sigma, which I had joined in the hope of finding some kind of home base.

In my fraternity house, the bathroom doors were large and swung both in and out—the sort they have in restaurants for busy waiters so nobody has to hold the door. Just push and go in. Push and come out. It was so simple; if only life's hard choices moved in the same way. Both of the bathrooms upstairs in the residential portion of the Kappa Sigma house had these doors. We referred to the bathrooms as the "front head" and the "back head" as if we were on a ship. The uses and origins of vaguely homoerotic terms in a house full of mostly straight eighteen- to twenty-two-year-old men were practically endless, but that one always struck me. Inside were stalls, urinals, and a gigantic group shower area. At varying intervals on any given day, the house intercom would blare "Beer shower!" and a dozen or so guys ran to the bathrooms, stripped naked, turned on the showers, and stood there drinking beer. I never did this, and to this day, I still can't imagine why they did, but they did.

My junior year, I lived in a single room three doors from the back head next to the fire exit. Life at USC might have been very different from my life in Indiana, but the desire to be near the exit to flee was a product of my wretched childhood. Practically speaking, it also made escaping the house and its occupants easier. In the end, I grew close to a few brothers, Alex, Anand, and others, and tried to make a replacement family. But they were mostly children of privilege, so that meant catering to their expectations—in many inconvenient ways, especially as official social chair for the house.

Being social chair seemed like a natural evolution. Since high school, I had been reinventing myself, even if I was never really me. Now, I gave the appearance of an extrovert who could throw the best parties, bring people together, and help them have fun, or at least get black-out drunk...you know, "fun" in 2002 collegiate sense. If that was what I had to do to be "needed," to be liked—hell, even to just have some minor value—fine. In a house of lazy, barely adult men, there were not many who wanted the job of planning events and dealing with the police if needed. With a dearth of takers, I fell into the position of party planning czar through self-selection. While I got to feel the purpose I craved so desperately, it also meant that every walk through the house was filled with "bros" offering unsolicited advice for the next party, street closures, buying out the Hotel Figueroa for a formal dance, or other unlikely scenarios. Getting drunk was one of three key priorities for the house's members. Making that happen was an actual job, and it came with reduced rent and free food, two critically important factors in my still impoverished state. I relished being needed, even if it was mercenary, but there were also times the back door out of the house was perfect, when I didn't feel like dealing with anyone.

The back door's greatest use was to escape the "the drop-in." A great deal of college is getting to know people living in close quarters, and the people I lived with took the term "fraternity brother" most seriously when drunk. At any moment, your door might burst open to reveal some bros with a drink asking to sit down for impromptu chats about feelings. Whoever thinks young men don't talk about their feelings has not spent enough time with them hopped up on tequila sunrises and vodka tonics. My room held the house's alcohol, so it was always a target, if only for a top-off. Until I convinced everyone to convert an old phone booth into the alcohol closet, the back door was my best escape from being interrogated about a life I was trying to forget. A quick pour, a few choice questions, and a handy escape route saved me from the constant fear of being discovered to be an imposter. An imposter with no social skills. An imposter with no money. An imposter with a sexuality that I was only just discovering.

My priorities in life till then could be summed up by how many nights I woke up with hunger pains, so sexual attraction had long been buried. I pushed it down so deep it's almost unbelievable it ever resurfaced or that I actually felt it when it did. Biology is a wonder that never ceases to amaze me, and in my life, it came out because of someone named James.

James was from Pi Kapp, a rival house down the "Row," the street that contained the sororities, fraternities, and morning-after walks of shame. I remember meeting him; it was the first day of writing class in the spring of junior year. We had both fought to get the class. The writing teacher, whose name I've forgotten, was known for being "cool" and "different," and his class was capped at twenty-five students. As he handed out syllabi and reviewed the semester with effortless flair, James and I exchanged glances of mutual admiration. We had gamed the system to gain entry to this class, even if only in ways that mattered to college juniors.

As we left class, we introduced ourselves. He was wearing a backwards navy-blue baseball cap, a look I generally disliked but did not mind on him. He was friendly, with piercing green eyes and an earnest kindness that was uncommon in this wealthy school. He asked if I had lunch plans in the non-committal way someone does when they're afraid of rejection, but I was not going to say "no." A few moments later, we were seated in a courtyard, eating club sandwiches, something I didn't admit I couldn't really afford. The sense of connection was strong enough I didn't mind missing the free lunch at my fraternity just to sit with James on the off chance of making an actual friend. We laughed and made small talk, like what classes we were taking, our majors, and how we managed to score a spot in the writing class. I don't remember what we said, which is unusual for me. What I do remember is the sunshine and the backwards baseball cap.

It never really dawned on me I might be feeling an attraction to James. It never occurred to me before to question my sexuality, or his, or anyone else's for that matter. I had grown up in rural Indiana, where there was little social diversity, let alone gay people. I didn't have a TV to see a future friend of mine "come out" on MTV. Gay did not exist for me, and the national news was not filled with stories about the sexually fluid-spectrum teenagers today get. I just thought I was making a real friend outside of a bar or fraternity, and that was enough for me. That *meant* something to me.

Proximity breeds closeness, which means college relationships, even platonic ones, can move fast. After three weeks, James and I were walking to class together, dining at each other's houses (a rare privilege), and spending every other night palling around campus bars. Weekends started on Thursday; we'd bounce from his house to mine doing shots. Thanks to my being social chair, we had unlimited access to the "good stuff," which meant liquor that didn't come in a plastic bottle. The other nights, James was at his house or his girlfriend's, and I was doing the same, minus the girlfriend. Most of my college days and nights blend together, a blur I'd be hard-pressed to recount except for the pang of true happiness I felt every time I spied that backwards baseball cap. A few moments do stand out: meeting his girlfriend, Jessica, who let slip that James could not shut up about the cool guy in his class he had become friends with; the first time I saw him without a hat (I discovered his hair was longer and lighter brown than I had imagined); and his heart-breaking birthday later that spring, which would be the last time I saw him.

In college, four months can be an eternity, so by late April, with finals approaching, it felt like I had known James forever. One day, he looked particularly frustrated. His birthday was approaching and, not being a child of privilege (another thing that connected us), he was limited in his options to celebrate with friends.

"Our house party is on Friday night. Why don't you just bring everyone there?" I suggested. In the fraternity world, this was a choice offer. The parties thrown by houses had strict guest lists, and I knew because I enforced ours. Girls were allowed in, but guys had to be on a "house list" of friends. Every member was allotted five slots so your party didn't turn into a "sausage party" or some other descriptive currently derided. But as social chair, I had access to my own unlimited guest list, and I was offering it for the most important party of the year. It's funny how important minor privileges can be in the small worlds we create for ourselves.

At USC in the spring, everyone would start to get anxious for exams they hadn't studied for or summer internships they hadn't lined up yet. As a result, fraternities always chose the two final weekends of the semester for a series of parties to blow off steam. Social chairs coordinated who got which Friday and which Saturday to avoid the Row looking like a war zone littered with Solo cups and ambulance rides for stomach pumps, all just inside the University's tolerance limit for alcohol abuse. These were opportunities to show off, and our house got Friday night with a fire and ice theme. I gave James a grand description of what we had planned: dry ice rooms, a private "members only" bar with no line and better alcohol, real fire dancers...the stuff of low-budget college dreams.

"Are you sure?" he asked. "I promise it wouldn't be more than like ten guys max, but that's a lot."

"Of course," I said, flexing the only power I had, one earned by keeping my bros drunk every week. "I'm social chair. I can let anyone I want in."

That weekend arrived, and I had the house on double-work duty. Everyone complained about the endless tasks, but I knew what I was doing. We were an up-and-coming house, and we needed to be successful to build our reputation. If I had learned one thing by this point after a second reinventing, it was that you had to plan for every moment you wanted. You had to claw your way out of the basement into freedom, into the world everyone else seemed to enjoy so easily. New fraternity pledges were putting up crepe paper all day, and older house members were making containers for the dry ice and hanging Visqueen plastic over the windows (before we knew how flammable all that shit was). While the rest of the house was stocked with Popov, Gordon's, and Wild Turkey, I set up the "bro bar" and its "prestigious" glass bottles of Absolut, Jack, and Tanqueray. I also made sure the bartenders knew there were bottles of Grey Goose for me and my guests, a special surprise for James and his friends.

As his arrival to the party drew closer, updates from James came in a stream of text messages: "Just finishing dinner with everyone, be there in an hour." "On our way, so stoked you're making this happen." "There's an eleventh guy, are you sure it's okay? I promise we're bringing a bunch of girls too." The house filled with young women in too-short skirts and bros in untucked shirts. Drinks flowed, the dance floor became sticky with spilt liquor, and no one thought to care. It was the epitome of a "hot" party, and everyone inside was happy. I nervously waited outside to greet James and his friends.

They arrived right on time, mostly because he continued texting me updates every five minutes. "Leaving PiKapp now." "One block away." "I see you!" I brought them in and handed my clipboard over to Pledge Class Apprentice Social Chair Nick, a freshman in training for when I relinquished the throne.

"I'm going in with my friends for a bit," I warned him. "Here's the list. We're full unless someone's on it. Don't fuck it up, or I will come back out here and break this shit over your head." Nick was properly terrified, as he had been trained to be, even though I did not indulge in our well-known hazing practices. James, Jessica, and the last of his friends strolled in with me.

As James headed to the bar, I stopped him and Jessica. "Wait, I have something for you." I slid "bro" wristbands on their arms, and I explained their privileges as if I were lord of the manor. "We don't have to drink that crap," I said, moving away from the main bar, as if I had come from a family that could even afford that "crap." We headed to my special "bro bar." The bartenders saw they were my guests and poured generously. From the dance floor to the bar then from the bar to the dance floor and back, and again and again.... It was a party's cycle of music, drinking, and dancing but this time with a best friend and his girlfriend.

Had I known then what I do today or had I been more experienced or more self-aware, I *might* have noticed something change as James got drunker. I *might* have seen the signals right there in front of me. But I wasn't, so I didn't. When red flags started going up, I didn't see them.

Jessica left to talk to some other friends, so James and I went to get refills. At the bar with no one around, we ordered three more vodka cranberries. As the bartender turned away, I felt someone ever-so-quickly grab my ass. I was used to pranks in the house, and I spun around looking for the culprit, but there was no one nearby.

"Everything okay?" James asked.

"Yeah, nothing," I said offhandedly. "Just someone being stupid…I don't know."

If I could go back in time, I'd scream in my own ear, "Look what's going on, put two and two together, you idiot!"

We headed back to the dance floor, found Jessica, and got back to the party cycle. As the three of us were dancing together, James slid Jessica between him and me, "Get Low" throbbing on the speakers. The three of us danced together, moving to the rhythm that filled the room. I thought it was just the usual "partying," until I felt James reach over Jessica's body and hold my waist. "He's just drunk," I thought to myself, "just holding on for balance," as we got down lower, and so I copied him. We danced like that, the three of us together holding each other, until the beat changed. Jessica had kept dancing the whole time; she hadn't reacted at all. Now I get it, of course, but back then I didn't see it, or I didn't want to see it. I still don't know which, but I had just sent James a major reciprocating signal without having any idea what I was doing.

The night hit maximum capacity around one a.m. The bar was crowded, the dance floor was wall-to-wall bodies, so everyone was touching someone, and the bathroom lines were long, all indicators I had put on a good party according to house standards. Jessica said she had to go to the bathroom and went off looking for the endless women's room line. To be heard over the music, I leaned in close to James and told him I was going upstairs to a private area of the house to use a different bathroom. During parties, we kept people downstairs, blocking off the second floor living area, both to keep everyone and the house safe and to contain the party downstairs so the bros didn't head back up to their rooms too early. But since I was running the place, I could go anywhere I wanted, and I was going to use that power to bypass a huge line at the men's bathroom.

"Wait," James insisted, "I don't want to wait in line, either. I'll come with you."

Drunk and high from the feeling of making my best friend happy, I swept us past security and down a deserted hallway. The security guys had been doing their job; it was just the two of us back there in the darkness.

We walked past the front head and towards the one near my room. For me, it was just force of habit, but to James it was a sign that we were thinking the same thing. I was inadvertently opening the door to his drunken impulse. We entered the bathroom and used the urinals almost in silence. We could hear the music from downstairs. James left before me, pushing the swinging door, walking out. I finished, glanced in the mirror as I washed my hands, and followed him out.

No sooner had I cleared the door before I was pushed quickly against the wall. It wasn't violent, and I wasn't scared, but I was surprised. It happened very quickly, but I remember every moment, and it still feels like an eternity. First, I realized it was James, pressing me up on the wall, holding my waist, not my arms. His green eyes flashed brightly under his shaggy hair, which had grown longer over the semester. It jutted out from the brim of that damn backwards baseball cap.

A quick look, just for a split-second from him, to confirm I was not scared or disgusted, and he leapt in for a kiss. It was short, it was deep, and it was passionate. I kissed him back, and I felt our tongues touch. This was *new*; this was incredible. I had made out with girls and even nearly "gotten to home plate," as is crassly said, but nothing had ever felt like this single kiss. All the chemistry, spark, and connection between us was transformed in this single simple action. It didn't last long as James moved away slightly, staring into my eyes. I stood there filled with passion, wonder, and fear. I was not expecting this to happen—I was never expecting to be kissed in general—but *that* night at *that* moment from James, my head almost exploded. So, I froze, and the kiss lingered in the air for a timeless instant.

Had I said anything other than what I did say, or maybe said nothing at all and kissed him back…almost anything different from what I had done, we might have found ourselves rushing madly to my room, fumbling with each other's clothes, and navigating the perils of a college romance as we both figured out how to come out of the closet and embrace our true selves together. If I had said something like, "My room's three doors down, let's go," I might have avoided years of dysfunctional relationships and continual emotional trial and error and become the poster boy for healthy gay marriage with two kids and a picket fence. The possibilities are almost endless. Those were the dreams I used to construct whenever I thought of my botched reaction to this lost pivotal opportunity in my life. I don't anymore. I was not a player and was too surprised to imagine any next step. So, in my lost and confused state, I said the first practical thing that came to mind: "Wait," I said without thinking, "ah, it's your birthday…uh…and your girlfriend is downstairs."

James immediately dropped his hands and stepped back. I can still see the sudden red flush in his cheeks and a disconcerted expression. As he saw things, I had let him grab my ass, we held each other on the dance floor, I brought him upstairs to be alone, and I had kissed him back. I could see him trying to understand what was happening, replaying in a nanosecond all the signals I had given him over the course of the night. He was trying to figure out why at that moment I would bring up his girlfriend when it was very clear what he wanted. Nearly dumbstruck and not wanting to visibly freak out, he stammered, "Um…yeah." Crestfallen, he said, "We should get back downstairs."

We walked more quickly than normal, but not running, as we returned downstairs to the party. We got on the dance floor again but remained safely apart. I kept going over everything in my mind. I was confused, but I was also electrified. I didn't really comprehend all of the implications of what had passed between us. But after thinking a moment, I realized I wanted more, in the same way that after an argument you belatedly have a perfect retort you wish could go back and say. In some doomed, awkward manner, I tried to get James alone again or send a signal without his girlfriend noticing. Not knowing what else to do, I offered to get everybody more drinks and went to the bar. James and Jessica stayed on the dance floor, and when I returned, they were nowhere in sight.

In a sort of a daze, I handed off the drinks to some random girls only too happy to take them in an innocent, trusting way no girl ever should. I kept my drink. I searched every room downstairs, found nothing, and then went to the main bar—not there, either. It didn't take long to see they had left. As far as I was concerned, that was it…done. The party was over. I was crushed. I handed off closing down the place to Nick the Pledge and slunk back to my room. I sent a safe text to James for fear of appearing to be a complete idiot: "Hey! It was so awesome to have you here for your birthday. Really looking forward to hanging out again. Grab a bite tomorrow?" He didn't respond that night or all weekend. I sent a few more texts, curious but not crazy, asking if everything was okay.

In my own head, I knew what was happening. As quickly as I had imagined a life for us together in just a few moments, confused as I was, I now knew I had lost an opportunity and I was losing a friend at the same time. Worst of all, I had ruined it myself by saying the wrong thing. James had risked everything, and how had I rewarded him? By crushing his feelings and accidentally threatening to out him to his girlfriend? But I was trapped. I was not ready to out myself to anyone, and I needed the friend I had just lost. James was not just my best friend; he was my only real friend. Now I had no one to talk to, and chasing him down might fracture a fragile sense of self for both of us. I wish I could say I was emotionally mature; I wasn't—I was just afraid.

When James did not show up to the last class we had together the next week, I knew it was over, but I didn't know how over. My calls went unanswered, and the other PiKapps I knew didn't have any idea where he was. They hadn't seen much of him either—everyone had figured it was just because of finals. I thought maybe he would reach out after a little bit. I told myself maybe our friendship wasn't totally lost. Maybe there was still a chance. I decided to wait it out.

I was not struggling with my sexuality, and I was not confused. I was just completely purpose-driven. It did not even dawn on me that I was gay; I just felt stuff for James. I was not crazy or crazed; I just wanted to talk to him. I missed him. I missed us, even the "us" that didn't kiss. When your world is shaken, I suppose, sometimes your brain gives reality to you in bite-sized, excruciatingly painful pieces.

During the end of finals, the Greek party line—a communications network of gossip, whispers, and rumors that kept the Row informed—finally carried me news of James's fate in the most innocuous way. In the middle of a lunch conversation with a bro, a friend with him asked, "Hey, weren't you friends with James?" I nodded but didn't say anything, looking down to avoid giving anything away. He followed up, "Do you know what happened to him?"

I looked up, suddenly surprised one last time by my absent friend.

"What do you mean?" I said.

"Oh, yeah, he was in my house," the visiting PiKapp said. "But as soon as he finished his finals, he up and left. He didn't tell any of us. Then we just got a notice yesterday during house renewals he's not coming back. Apparently, he moved home or something? Just transferred out in the middle of the night, basically, and hasn't responded to anyone."

"Oh, uh, no," I answered. "I haven't heard from him either." I took my plate, got up as quickly as possible, and left, trying to make it look like I wasn't really affected by the news.

As I fell down on my bed, I realized what had happened. I didn't message James telling him I'd heard he had left. I didn't send an email confessing my love in a last great display of emotion. I didn't even call to leave a final voicemail. I did what I had been trained to do my entire life in the face of loss. I accepted it in tears, alone in my room. I moved on, no matter how hurt.

The back head would just once more come into my life in a transformative way. That summer, I was still living in the fraternity house and working at DreamWorks in a coveted paid internship at one of Hollywood's top studios. An assistant three cubicles overtook a liking to me. He tried to draw me out, little by little, over instant messenger.

"Have you ever been with a guy?"

"No."

"Would you like to be with one?"

"I don't know."

"It doesn't mean you're gay if you do."

"I know."

"Would you let me go down on you?"

No response.

"Did I go too far? Sorry, I didn't mean to offend you."

"You didn't."

"So…would you?"

I let him go down on me later that summer. He had invited me over to his apartment, and I drank as many apple-tinis as he made me, as fast as I could, as we watched *Down with Love*. The first time he touched my hand, I recoiled. The second, I let him move his hand across my arm to below my waist. We had sex. It was all meaningless to me at the time. I wanted to experience it, I told myself. So, this was how you "experience" these things, I figured. I did not tell him he was the first guy I had sex with or that he was destined to be a one-night stand.

The situation was all just "fine" until it wasn't. As we lay there in his apartment, he whispered sweet nothings in my ear and committed what would become the cardinal sin for anyone who wanted me to care about them. He told me he liked me, he told me I was smart, he wanted to date me, and I could be his boyfriend. Suddenly, it was all too much.

I was overwhelmed. I couldn't breathe. I couldn't imagine life as a gay man. This was not just about James anymore, this was a life, a road from which there was no return. I raced to put my clothes on, mumbling some excuse about it being late, and ran out the door without so much as a goodbye.

I panicked the entire way home, heaving and coughing as if my body was trying to expel some terrible poison. The moment I crashed through the back door, a quick way in as it was out, I ripped off my clothes and ran for the showers. I was usually fearful of anyone else being there, but this time I didn't even bother to look. I turned the shower on as hot as I could get it and knelt on the floor. I heaved and threw up everything inside me as I convulsed. I sat there for half an hour, naked on the tile floor, steam gathering around me, trembling and throwing up like I never had before in my life. Whatever was in the pit of my stomach, my body wanted out, but it was no use. You can't throw up who you are inside. It was change, it was James, it was my family, it was the crush of another loss, and it was the realization that I was gay; it all felt like a gigantic setback in my lifelong quest to feel like someone who was like everyone else…anyone else. And it wasn't going to go away no matter how much I choked.

Suddenly, I wasn't just poverty-stricken, or weird, or lonely, or friendless, I was different in who I was attracted to, as well. It was too much. I dry-heaved until my abs ached from the pain, but I kept going, coughing and crying until another bro, also staying in the house that summer, stumbled in to urinate in the middle of the night. He asked me if I was okay, and I didn't say anything. He had the good sense not to question me anymore, and he left. Immediately, I realized I had to stop; I forced myself to stop shaking and convulsing by sheer will. I stood up, turned off the shower, and retreated back to my room.

As I lay there on my cheap Wal-Mart cotton sheets, wetness spreading through the pillowcases, I stared at the empty bunk above mine. I plotted and planned against a future I was going to try to prevent. And I cried and cried. I cried for things I had lost and things I had not experienced: the comforting sameness of a couple on a wedding cake, the ease with which others navigated relationships by falling in and out of bed in a world of mutual collegiate escapist promiscuity, and any hope of being normal. Those things had been completely washed away. All because of a first kiss in the back of my fraternity house one spring night. Goddammit.

CHAPTER 8

THE LAST CHRISTMAS

My bathroom breakdown and crushing sense of loneliness did not inhibit my continuing attempts to build a fake life at USC, even with massive hiccups along the way. If I could not be who I wanted to be, I was going to redouble my efforts to pretend I was like everyone else. I was living in two realities at once. I kept the real one at bay and instead threw party after party—hung out with all the bros, underscoring for me what was becoming a brilliant ability to compartmentalize. I turned back to the grind of school and could momentarily lose myself in the fiction I had created. However, I was brutally reminded of my origins and who I truly was when I took an ill-advised trip home to Greensburg for the last time.

Divorces are almost always messy. So why should one from your parents be any different? Though I had been disowned many years before, I couldn't cleanly cut these ties cold turkey. Though I received no help from these wayward "former parents," there were times when I almost wished things could have gone right. No matter how horrific they were or had been, there was still an innocence in me that hoped for some miraculous change in our relationship. It seemed no matter how far I ran, and I had run all the way to California, I could not cut the ties that bound me to my past. What I would have given for Atropos to take pity on me. Instead, her sisters continued spinning my thread longer and longer but always anchored to Greensburg. So, when, after months of handwringing, Joan suggested that I visit for Christmas, I reluctantly accepted the offer in a bout of what must have been emotional insanity. The trip would finally cure me of hoping for any remaining tie to these people who once would have been called, however ill-fitting, family and sever my connections once and for all.

There I was, on a cold December day after the fall semester of senior year, standing in front of the cobalt-colored plexiglass deli counter at the Super Wal-Mart in Greensburg. I had come to see my "family," but I shouldn't have. I stared at the at the flat, open-air display case filled with sandwiches like those I had seen hundreds of times before and was triggered. I had spent almost every day during high school staring at this counter, trying to choose what to eat while on break. But every day, it was the same thing: the signature "Po' boy." These are not the Po' boys of TripAdvisor's best foods of New Orleans; no, these were large, tube-shaped, white-bread hoagies filled with bland shaved turkey. Priced to move at $1.84, I could buy a sandwich and split it in half, providing food for two meals instead of just one. It wasn't really a choice; it was all I could do. Food did not fill an emotional gap or bring me pleasure; I didn't feel the way other people did at the joy of a delicious meal and a warm embrace. Like all of life's little joys, I was deprived of that kind of experience. Food was just a means to an end, a practical choice that had to be carried out, and a subject of stress, not pleasure.

After scarfing my sandwich down, I'd rush back to work at the department store for another series of choices that were really about what had to be done in order to survive because living with Joan and Dale, even in the basement dungeon, provided me a steady diet of selfishness, bad parenting, homegrown vegetables, and expired steak. I had to fend for myself. After they disowned me, it was even worse—if I wanted to eat, I had to find it. What I needed to spend to survive, I had to earn. As a result, every day was a painful routine of rushing from school to work, where I managed the cash registers. The hours passed monotonously, folding sweaters, hanging shirts, and tendering discount corduroy and work boots that, even at rock-bottom prices, were too expensive for me to afford.

I lived and died by my employee discount, waiting until last the minute clearance markdowns in hopes something special might still be available in addition to the basics I needed to survive. It was always like that: hard choices. Which turkey sandwich had an ounce more meat? Which sweater was discounted deeply enough it hit the sweet spot between affordable and decent versus cheap and so garish no one else would buy it?

As I stood there in front of the deli counter many years later, remembering all those non-choices, the idea of having made progress at USC melted away in the bright fluorescent lights. I thought about buying one just for "old time's sake," but realized this would result in either needing the Heimlich maneuver or a clean-up on aisle six. I wandered past the rows of packaged food, deeper into the nether regions of the deli section. I ordered hot chicken nuggets, coleslaw (more mayo than cabbage), and barbeque sauce—an improvement, but not by much. I was twenty-one years old and continued to be boxed in by poverty's limitations. I could only fill myself with delusions of a somewhat limited grandeur. I was standing alone in a grocery store killing time waiting to drive out to my despised childhood home—not the best situation I had envisioned for my Christmas break.

Even when it seemed I was heading toward something better in Los Angeles, standing back in that Wal-Mart, the patron saint of Greensburg's poor and middle classes, brought me back to a harsh, unpleasantly lit reality. I threw away the rest of my meal and made for the door; my pit stop was over. I got in my car, off to travel the country roads until I drove back in time to a disturbing set of memories in the form of a brick house filled with chintz, trinkets, and people who did not love or care for me in any way.

It was near dark when I arrived. The rural twilight left nothing to the imagination where I lived. There are no streetlights in the countryside, and this year, the house was bereft of Dale's usual tradition of garishly hanging colored Christmas lightbulbs on any spot that could take a nail. This year, he was ill with testicular cancer, undergoing aggressive chemotherapy, and neither he nor anyone else felt like putting in the effort. As I pulled into the driveway a few days before Christmas, it struck me that I never understood why Dale put up lights at all. They certainly didn't look good. Our house was not one of joy or good cheer. We lived in the middle of nowhere. Christmas might be my favorite holiday now, but it certainly wasn't then. Instead, it was commemoration of expectations unmet, filled with cheap jewelry for my mother Joan and an odd assortment of gifts purchased from the twenty-four-hour gas station for my twin sister Carla and me. You really know your father is a drunk and a loser when he gives you batteries and a misshapenly-wrapped lighter in newspaper at thirteen years old. I did not smoke, and I could not afford anything that needed batteries.

That Christmas of 2003, I did not even expect bad gifts, and I hadn't brought any. After the fraught relationship I had with Dale and Joan, I had decided my presence was all they we going to get from me. This wasn't because I felt like I was anything special. I had simply reached the limit of my own sanity and depression. My family was a very fucked up place that fucked me up, if you haven't gathered that yet.

I walked through the front door, which was never locked, because there was nothing worth stealing. Dale barely acknowledged me from his recliner, where he might have been sitting for days, months, or years—there was no way to really tell. Chemotherapy or alcohol, it didn't matter; the only thing that had changed over the years was the fading of the chair's fake leather and the horrible carpet underneath. Joan greeted me with the most genuine hug a mother could give, which was unexpected, considering she had never acted like this before. She then ushered me to the first-floor guest bedroom that I had so unceremoniously been banished from many years before. How surreal, just two years after leaving for good, ten years after being sent underground, to be welcomed back into that house and given the room of honor, the bedroom I had been tossed out of as a child, as if nothing had ever happened. It was enough to make you want to eat a Po' boy from Wal-Mart in celebration…almost.

I said my goodnights and clicked off the lights, staring at the same 1978 encyclopedia volumes I had grown up reading, not knowing this would be the last time I'd stare at those faded books.

The next morning, there was a knock at the bedroom door. Carla, who was supposed to take Dale to chemotherapy, had instead disappeared to see some friends for day drinking at a local dive bar. With Dale out of other options, the request for a drive to cancer treatment fell on me. I don't know why, but I agreed.

The drive to the nearby "big city" of Columbus was silent, except for Dale muttering minimal directions. He was tired and scared, and I could tell. I learned that he had stopped drinking, though it wouldn't last long, and started attending mass daily instead of weekly. For him, it was a race to the finish line between life and death, and he was going to get every communion wafer from the hand of the local priest he could, in case the dice came up snake-eyes. I realized, from the few brief statements he shared, he was not scared of death per se—he was scared of what might happen after. It seemed as if his temporary sobriety had also left him with a conscience for the years of rampant abuse that he inflicted on everyone around him, including myself. A devout Catholic, Hell was on his mind. I, too, was Catholic then, but Hell was never at the center of my mind the way it appeared in the door waiting for him.

We barely said a word the whole ride, letting the crisp winter pass by silently. It was getting warmer during the day, which melted snow, but as night fell, the water would harden to ice. Nature seemed to have an odd sense of foreboding that day.

I don't really remember what I did while he got his treatment. I didn't sit with him. Columbus had a mall, so I probably wandered about at Fair Oaks, as it was called, searching for nothing and everything at the same time. I showed up at the appointed hour and picked Dale up, and we headed back on the half-hour drive home.

We made it nearly the entire way unscathed. Less than a mile from the house, however, we hit a patch of black ice. Growing up, the roads had been easier to navigate when they were dirt and gravel, but the county had apparently come into some money and decided to bring our neighborhood of three country houses into the late 20th century with some low-grade blacktop. So, no matter how carefully I drove, I was going to hit a patch of undetectable ice, and when I did, it sent the car spinning.

I held the car steady. I may have moved to Los Angeles, but I had spent eighteen years in Greensburg, and that was not the first nor last patch of black ice I'd hit. I often wonder what would have happened if I had just let go of the steering wheel. Would we have slammed into a ditch and simply walked away? Would the car have flipped and Dale, in his weakened state, bled out before help arrived? Suffice it to say none of that happened.

No sooner had I started and completed my correction, saving us from certain doom, than this sickly man in the car next to me sprung back to life. Sick from chemo, scared of Hell, barely conscious, he came to with the furor of the man I had grown up with. Dale was back. He was screaming at the top of his lungs, insulting me and berating me for being so stupid as to hit an unavoidable patch of ice. I was a pussy, an idiot, a complete waste of space. Here I was, driving him back from the very thing keeping him alive, and I was being berated for an act of charity I did not even know I was capable of. I don't raise my voice now, but I did then.

I bellowed at him with all the power, volume, and menace my twenty-one-year-old voice could muster, "Shut the hell up!"

And he did.

As we finished the remaining drive back to the house, we sat there saying nothing. I wanted to scream all sort of things at him. I wanted to ask him, if he were so afraid of Hell, why had it not occurred to him before that he shouldn't treat his own children worse than dogs? Why did he hate me so much? Why was I relegated to the basement? Why, if I brought so much misery into their lives, did they have me, and why did they give that hate back into my life tenfold? I had so much nuclear anger inside me at that moment, I felt I could melt the ice for miles around. I could feel everything I'd ever wanted to say, but worse, it made me even angrier at myself that I'd never said anything before. In all our fights, why hadn't I asked why? Why hadn't I told them before that they were awful parents? Why had I not reported them to authorities when I was left to fend for myself? Why did I cover for them? It seemed, at that moment, a lifetime of grief and anger had finally come through, and this cancer-riddled, crippled old man next to me was the source of much of the suffering I had experienced my whole life.

And so I broke. This was going to be the moment I finally spoke the horrible, awful truth of my life and my feelings about him. One advantage I have in life, partially thanks to years of subsequent obsessive practice, is a keen sense of how to gauge people's emotions. When you're poor, an outsider, a loser, you learn to read a room quickly, lest you make a mistake you can't fix. I had trained myself to read the faces around me for what they wanted to hear. It's a trait that, decades later, has made me empathetic to those around me, a better friend, and a better man when I'm smart enough to rely on it. I do not live in fear anymore, but I live conscious of others' emotions and how to help them if needed.

But in that moment with Dale, I did not have any impulse to offer him support. My baser instincts prevailed, and I used the same skill of reading faces to unleash a verbal torrent of cruelty as masterful as it was blunt. It didn't take much to read him and slice him open like the fish he used to steal from the pond next door every weekend growing up.

As I pulled his beaten-up, powder blue Ford Explorer into the garage, I let the door close behind us. He moved to open his car door, but I grabbed his arm and stopped him. He stared at me, feeble green eyes still filled with rage from his outburst just moments earlier but quickly fading. I said to him, with all the serenity and sincerity of a solemn Catholic beatitude, "I know that this cancer scares you. I know that you are afraid to die. And I know that *everyone* around you is *rooting* for you, *praying* for you to get through this." My voice was quiet but only to land a larger blow as I finished. "But I want you to know, I hope you die. Because then, you will go to the Hell that both you and I know you deserve."

Were Dale any ordinary man, he might have laughed it off. Had he been his drunken self, he might have yelled back at me, fighting off my words with a shield of insults. But he was broken, devout, and newly self-aware, if only barely. I knew this, and I knew my words would cut him deeply. He said nothing, shut the door, and sank back into the car seat. I got out and closed my door behind me.

As I walked through the house, Joan called out, "Where's your father?" and I told her he was sitting in the car. I didn't say why. I went to the guest room and began quietly packing my bags. I knew this was the end, and my time here was over. I was simply waiting for the fallout before departing.

It took the others about an hour to get him out of the car and another three before he told everyone what I had said. As the commotion began, but before the group that now included my older, adopted brother and sister and their families could confront me, I phoned Jim and Lacey to come get me.

Jim and Lacey were the parents of my childhood "hallway friend" Angie. Grown-ups I knew I could trust to help and support me in a time of need. I had never called on them for help before, but I felt I could in this moment. Angie's compassion in the hallways had been a reflection of their even greater and wiser virtues. Her parents and I had periodically kept in touch with a phone call every few months, more contact than I had with Angie. In college, they were still role models without equal. I was drawn to them; talking to them always brought me comfort and a belief that genuine kindness from an adult was possible. At the very least, I could get advice from people who knew how to give it. They were good parents and were the only people I knew in town.

I called Jim and simply said, "I'm at my parents' house. I need you to come get me. Don't ask any questions yet, please. Just come and get me as soon as possible. Be careful of the black ice." It was after midnight, but Jim simply said, like any loving parent would, "I'm on my way." No questions asked—the care and love for a human being came before anything else.

As I hung up the phone, I took my suitcase and opened the door to the guest room and started down the hallway. Dale, Joan, Carla, and the whole family were gathered together and were ready for a fight, but no one seemed to know how to start one without an accelerant like vodka, beer, or some nearly lethal potion called 151. So, they milled around for twenty minutes, feeding each other's illegitimate anger until they were ready to turn on me. They viciously unleashed a litany of complaints. "What's wrong with you? How could you? What an awful person." I felt nothing. I only asked if none of them remembered what life had been like. Have all of you simply accepted who he was as a person and moved on?

What I didn't say was "None of you were in that car. And none of you realize that he might look old and infirm now, but if he lives, he'll be back. He hasn't changed, he hasn't repented, he hasn't found Jesus. He has found motive. And while I may someday forgive him (and I would), I will never forget he is a soulless man who deserves to be pitched into the depths of Hell."

I didn't say that, but I should have.

Jeff, my oldest sibling, asked me to leave. I told him my ride was already on its way. I simply grabbed my suitcase and left without a word; Jim was outside in a few minutes. There was no point in saying I'd never return and no need for vindication or closure. I knew it, and that was good enough for me.

As we drove, Jim didn't ask what happened. I'm sure he could see it on my face. And for all the efforts at covering things up over the years, it was a small town, and he knew I was not leaving anything good that night. When a father brings his children to the bar and drinks all day because he can't paint houses in the rain, bartenders hear things that make their way around town. Surely, some of Dale's behavior and confessions had made it to Jim through the grapevine.

That Christmas Eve, I did not ask to stay with Jim and Lacey, and they did not invite me. It just happened. They simply brought me into their home without a word and into a bedroom decorated with fluffy pink satin frills and lace. At some point between my call and when I arrived, one of their daughters had moved to another room, made the bed, and prepared for my arrival. All without saying a word. Jesus Christ, that's high-level family-ing. Perhaps Angie and her sister were asleep or listening as I settled in for the night; their parents had probably said to give me some space.

When I woke on Christmas morning, I was given a plate and told to pile it high with eggs, pancakes, sausage, and more. I had rarely experienced such bounty. Then it was time to open presents. I was initially reluctant, stung by the painful feeling I was imposing on a family's holiday. I was an imposter, and there would be a reminder of that when they passed out presents, none of which could be for me. Lacey just piled more scrambled eggs onto my plate. It's a miracle I didn't burst into tears right then or moments later, when Jim called me to come to the Christmas tree.

"Craig, here, this one's got your name on it," he said so nonchalantly that his words nearly threw me backwards into their breakfast counter.

That was impossible.

I had arrived near one o'clock in the morning on Christmas day. I had not been planning on seeing Jim and Lacey, so advance preparation wasn't possible. But one after another, I opened several presents from them. One was a bottle of Calvin Klein cologne, something so expensive I would have never even considered getting it for myself. All the gifts were neatly wrapped, and just like Jim said, my name was actually on the tags. None of their kids said anything, and no one acted as if I should be anywhere else but in their home on Christmas. Maybe there was some midnight family meeting or Jim and Lacey had been driving for hours to find an open store—who knows. All I really know was that I felt the love and warmth of the best Christmas I had ever had. For a few blessed hours, I was in a true, honest-to-God home. They never asked what had happened or what my plans were. Hours later, when I had to go to the airport to catch a flight, they all seemed genuinely sorry to see me go. Jim drove me to the airport without question or complaint.

I knew they were not my family. I knew it was not the Christmas I had planned, but for a moment, it felt like it was.

That made everything all right in the world for a little while. I even remember laughing and feeling happy, though I couldn't tell you about what specifically. Through pure chance, I'd return to Greensburg once more in my life under very different circumstances, and that was just fine. That would always be fine after that Christmas. Other Christmases were coming in the future. They might come with heartbreak, joy, even loss or frustration. There was one with a blizzard. But most importantly, none came with batteries or lighters wrapped in newspaper again.

CHAPTER 9

THE COLLAPSE—TAKE I

Growing up with emotional terrorists as parents left me a shattered person chasing heedlessly after misshapen ideas about what it meant to be a teenager and then an adult. I thought at times I had thrived in spite of an absolutely crazy upbringing. But I was wrong—their complete lack of love and care left a gaping hole in my life. I was desperate to fill it with almost anything that even vaguely resembled that missing love and care...which always ended poorly.

At first, I did so in small ways: idolization of Mrs. Cash and emulating others who seemed willing, even in a small way, to be a friend. I risked everything for professors who looked and behaved like parents, but in the end, all I got was a pat on the head and a one-way ticket out of town, exiled to California. With James, I experienced something new: the passion and desire of romantic love. It was a different type of connection than I had felt before; it seemed more important than anything. Of course, I did not—could not—love someone I had I only known for a few months, but I had walked close to the fire and, like forbidden fruit, I wanted more.

Then fall of senior year, I fell in love for real. The loss of that love after my last Christmas in Indiana, when I needed it most, made the events at DePauw seem like minor setbacks. During my senior year at USC, I would have my heart broken, and I'd find myself at the brink of emotional and psychological collapse.

At the beginning of the year, things had started smoothly. I was king of the hill, even if only a small one. I was social chair at the fraternity, unrivaled in my ability to "keep the bros happy." Some had even begun to complain there were too many social events. When a group of eighteen- to twenty-two-year-old, red-blooded, all-American boys complain there is too much alcohol and too many girls around, you've done your job. I recruited record-breaking pledge class after record-breaking pledge class, catapulting my house from the bottom of the pecking order to just below the top tier. I was excelling in my classes, beloved by professors who praised my diligence and wondered at my combination of tenacity, charm, and frankness. I wrote my senior thesis in crayon and still earned a silver medal. Times were good, you might say, but only in the way a lot of frosting can mask a bad bake on a cake.

And I was a really, really bad bake. I had created and propped up the outward appearance of what I thought people wanted. But no amount of pretending could make me believe that person was me. In spite of my burgeoning homosexuality, I bedded girl after girl in an elaborate and unnecessary cover job. Jessica, Brie, Courtney, Katie, Tiffany, and another Jessica, their names running together as if chosen from a Stepford catalog. Perhaps more importantly, I secretly held, but did not act on, my attraction to Brandon, Tyler, and Tristan, another Brandon, James, and Michael.

The world I had been constructing was starting to show cracks in the façade and, worse, in its foundation. I may have helped my fraternity build its reputation, but resentment was building not-so-quietly around me as I also turned the house into a place that the people who lived there didn't recognize. They wanted a stereotypical fraternity experience. I had brought on professional chefs, tripled the social budget, threw parties with elaborate sets and decorations, and gave us a reputation for hard partying and access to Hollywood nightclubs. I lived a life I thought I wanted but did not enjoy. I did it with money I didn't have, living on credit cards I shouldn't have had. It all just felt so empty and pointless, but I was powerless and unable to stop.

The reality was I didn't have anything else except this precarious existence. I needed to believe in the work I was doing and the life I was building because of the absence of any real connection. It was all just one cover-up after another to compensate for the void at the center of my soul, and my mind raced at night as a result. I started taking Unisom to fall asleep, but even that had limited utility. Still, I would not give in to the debilitating despair, even with all the signs of crisis in my life. I vowed I would force life to happen the right way when it didn't happen on its own. I would make this all work. I thought I could convince everyone, including myself.

Only years later would I realize people were not as naïve as I believed at the age of twenty-one. People sensed an inauthenticity about me, even if they couldn't put their finger on it, and they hated me for it. Those who were their most authentic, egregious, and awful selves all the time hated me most.

Enter Omid, a fraternity brother who had pledged the same time as I had. Omid was considered the diamond in the rough of our fraternity but only if that diamond were made of cheap glass, had a toxic personality, and possessed a level of self-hatred equal to my own. But where I had buried my sense of loss and failure in an attempt to look and act like everyone else, Omid had instead compensated with a brooding, crass honesty and sense of over-familiarity. For him, everyone in our pledge class was his true brother, everyone in the house his true family, but anyone who did not adopt the same creed was a traitor and a danger. As a social animal hellbent on popularity over familiarity, on parties over real connections, I was Omid's foil, and everyone knew it, including us. Given his druthers, he would do whatever he wanted to me, like a human punching bag or rag doll. Fortunately, my value to the house stood in his way, as well as a vague sense of right and wrong and perhaps a rough understanding of the laws on assault and battery. His inability to bring me down only increased his animus, and my position in the house system drove him to the brink of insanity. Omid was a tectonic fault that would violently shift with five-point Richter-scale acts when drunk.

If Omid was the destructive wave I saw coming my way, Andrew was the salve I had not. In the midst of my toxic caldron of feelings, mistakes, rivalries, successes, and attempts to fit in, he unexpectedly took center stage. He provided me with the revelation of what it truly meant to love and be loved. I would, for the first time, briefly understand what it was like to fill the void in my soul, even if just a little.

I met Andrew in the fall of 2003 during Rush week. An endless series of parties and expensive nights out, Rush week was also about discerning what a "pledge" wanted most in the world and promising to get it. If anyone was good at figuring out what someone wanted and becoming that, it was me. I always stood out during Rush as everyone's favorite brother. If you loved tennis, "Let me introduce you to Charlie. He owns three tennis courts at his house in Connecticut, you should go there sometime." If you had never kissed a girl, "Meet my friend Katherine, she'll show you a *very* good time." If you were socially awkward and loved to get high, "Tommy here will show you to his room. He has the latest *Grand Theft Auto* and really good shit."

Then there was Andrew, or Andrew Russ, as he insisted he be called, to differentiate himself from his unpleasant, over-bearing father of the same name back in Ohio. Right from the get-go, that told me all I needed to know about Andrew. I plied him with promises of making him BMOC with the grandeur and celebrity of my job in Hollywood. I invited him to a red-carpet premiere, where he was surrounded by people who were attracted to his devilish good looks and aww-shucks charm. I took the things he'd always seen and loved in himself but was afraid to let out, and I made them stand out. And for that, he loved me and the house. He pledged as part of another record-breaking class, and though he was two years younger and three years behind me in school, we both felt a deep electricity between us.

At the beginning I was resistant, not knowing what it was. Attempting real connections had not gone well so far. The only one I had known ended in a tragically wonderful kiss and a heartbreaking departure. The rest were just drunken conversations that threated to expose my vulnerabilities and weaknesses. I did not allow others to really know me—hell, I didn't really know myself. But Andrew was persistent, he was earnest, and he was beautiful. And I came to realize he was also in trouble and hurting. As far as I knew, I had never met someone who was troubled in the same way I was.

Our real story began three weeks into his pledge semester. He unexpectedly showed up at my door in the middle of the night, backpack in hand. Had I known the future, I really don't know what I would have done. All I knew then was he looked like he needed some help, and my past life had made me very sensitive to people who needed help.

"Can I stay here for the night?" he shyly asked. I was stunned. "I don't have anywhere else to go," he earnestly pleaded. I quickly welcomed him into my room with no idea what a big change that small act would lead to.

"I don't understand...don't you have a dorm room?" I queried. Every freshman was required to live in campus housing, and Andrew was a freshman, so I didn't know what was going on.

He told a tale of woe I could relate to. His roommate had "sexiled" him, a term for locking the door to have sex and leaving your roommate out in the cold. Tonight was the third time this week. Even when Andrew was in his room, his roommate berated him, hassled him, smelled, took his stuff, ate his food, and generally terrorized him. It had been three weeks of hell, according to him, and it was not getting better. The upper-class supervisor was unwilling or unable to step in, and Andrew didn't know what to do. He couldn't focus in class, hadn't had a good night's sleep in weeks, and was effectively homeless. If I hadn't understood where he was coming from, I might have thought he was reverse-Rushing me, hitting every soft spot I had.

I showed him to the couch and told him he was welcome to spend the night. The sofa was not very comfortable, I warned him; it was a hand-me-down from the prior occupant, and I couldn't afford a new one, so I had kept it. Now, at least, for Andrew, it was a quiet place to sleep. As he fell asleep, I did too, smiling at my generosity. What an unusual position I was in, as I rarely had the resources or desire to be authentically generous to anyone. My entire life had focused on survival, playing a role, and being the person others wanted me to be. I had listened to the bros when they cried about breakups but never felt their pain. I set them up with new girlfriends, never really understanding their joy. I had hosted amazing parties for others, but I never had fun at them. Here, I brought a stray in, and for the first time, I could feel his relief. It was new, and it was addictive.

When Andrew woke the next morning, he asked if he could stay another night until he could sort out his roommate situation. A few days at most, he said. I was reluctant because fraternizing with pledges was frowned upon, but I agreed out of a sense of concern. He had pulled on all the right heartstrings—he was in need with no way out, and I knew what that felt like. I told myself he could slip in and out of the back door at night, and if I hid the situation well enough from everyone else, no one would ever be the wiser.

Return he did, night after night. At first, he was still "living" in his dorm; he almost never had a change of clothes when he arrived. Soon, however, we both grew more comfortable with the situation. In a few weeks, a small pile of his clothes sat innocently enough in the corner of the room. We spent all our time together and would fall asleep after talking until the early morning hours. I can't remember a time when I got so little sleep but felt so awake and alive.

Soon, he turned around and was sleeping on the couch with his head resting up against mine on the edge of my pillow, the couch having been pushed up against the head of my bed. In fact, for a person who did not like to be touched and hated when someone touched my head, I became unable to sleep unless our heads were next to each other. Sometimes, his hand would reach out and touch my shoulder or face. While we were still sleeping with girls—young men mired in denial will cling to any cover story—we embraced a Greek sense of romance. And in that sense, it was romantic, a relationship without physical sex but built with emotional strands that felt like bungee cords of strength. I was in heaven, and I felt a sense of peace I had never known.

Our late-night conversations went for hours. At first, only he was doing the sharing. About his brothers. His father. A woman he called his foster mother, who took care of him when no one else would. The high school swim team, his freshman classes…every detail of his life. He abandoned all caution and threw an unbridled sense of vulnerability out into the open as he shared every detail and feeling. I had met someone who was so open, but he clearly wanted me to reciprocate. I resisted initially, but even the strongest fish in the pond is worn down by a careful reel in and out over time.

Little by little, I opened up. I talked about the family that raised me and how they treated me. About the overwhelming depression I felt every day, something we both knew. My hopes for making it out alive and making it big, something we also shared. I don't think we would have grown as close if his family had money or had he not known true hardship. But he was a lost soul like me, even if he had been rescued much earlier than I was. He even introduced me to "Lori," a legend in his hometown. A woman of kindness and generosity like I had never experienced before. She was his confidant, his mentor, and his caretaker. She was his unofficial foster mother. I would learn she played that role for other members of Andrew's high school swim team, back in Perrysburg, Ohio. She sent him money and gifts, as other parents did to their college-bound children, and soon enough, she sent things to me, as well. No one had ever sent me gifts ever. I didn't even know what to do, but Andrew made sure I kept the shirt and shoes. He had told Lori of my plight, my miserable situation amplified by my taped-up sneakers. She insisted that every man should have a good pair of dress shoes. She was Italian, after all, and she cleaved close to that heritage.

Our nights together quietly became weeks, and even the house's harassment of pledges during the final days of the semester did not hinder the growth of our bond. When Andrew went home for Thanksgiving break, he called every day and we talked for hours, extending our connection over thousands of miles. He vented about how his family treated him, leapt with excitement that Lori wanted to meet me, and wondered aloud when we would see each other again, even though we had been apart for just a few days. It would be years before I looked back on this experience and saw it for what it really was: my first true love, and his too, I think. It would be years before I would see the more problematic parts: my using the relationship to compensate for the gaps in my life rather than fix them and his using this relationship to leapfrog to the front of the line. It was a quickly growing attachment that was so fast and so strong that neither of us bothered to closely examine our motives or their ramifications on the other. In the moment, all that mattered was my attachment to Andrew and his to me. He was someone who knew me, the true me, and still want to be around me. We called each other best friends, but there was an ever-present undercurrent. Only twice did those unspoken emotions ever manifest physically, although at different times for each of us.

It came first for me. Andrew and I had planned to hang out together, but he didn't show up. Our bond was intense and unhealthy, so even the smallest slight could become a major source of anxiety. I sent a few texts but received nothing in return. I tried to chalk it up to a missed connection, but Andrew had been insistent on supporting me in my latest crisis. I had been unusually stressed about work and money. I had received bad news that day: I wasn't getting the raise I needed from my job to survive, and money was running out, credit cards notwithstanding. He vowed to be there for me, and when he didn't arrive, I did something I had not done in months: I grabbed a bottle of sleeping pills and took a few, just to relax and get some sleep. The bottle said, "Two pills every six to eight hours," or something safe like that, I'm sure. But by this point, my personal dose had increased to a handful. An hour later, I still could not sleep. It was barely seven o'clock, and my body would not let me. I took another handful. I lay back down.

My phone buzzed. On high alert, waiting to hear from Andrew, I grabbed it, but it wasn't him. It was the all-Greek organization committee I was chair of; a board meeting was about to start, and they did not take kindly to my being late, or worse, not showing up. Maybe it would distract me, I thought. I dragged myself out of bed to the Kappa Delta Delta Sorority House. Had my room been further than few steps from the back door or had KDD not been directly across the street, I likely would have passed out in a hallway or bush somewhere. But by some small miracle, I made it to KDD and sat silently on a red poufy couch, waiting to be called on for my report. I was not tired, but my mind was hazy. When it was my turn to go, I stood to speak and lost consciousness.

It wasn't the nice "happy drunk" type of pass out where you stay asleep. It was an "I took too many sleeping pills" sort of pass out. I fell and hit my head on an end table. Helicopter mothers with a fragile two-year-old are second only to well-heeled, over-privileged sorority girls in their ability to erupt into a panic, and my collapse was enough to send everyone into a tizzy. My fraternity brothers were quickly summoned, as I attempted some semblance of coherence. I had to be practically carried back to the fraternity house, stumbling and staggering with faltering steps. I fell down not once but twice on the stairs as I was helped up to my room.

I was always well put together, so even a bunch of irresponsible twenty-year-olds will find it jarring when they see the person who is usually so composed falling down the stairs at eight o'clock without a drop of alcohol in his system. Still, they did not call the hospital. In retrospect, I know it was it was not naiveté but a well-understood and unwritten rule: fraternities never called authority figures of any kind to their houses. Adults made things worse, and more importantly, all the other infractions in plain sight would suddenly be brought to light at the same time. I lay on my bed, I don't know for how long, having lost all sense of the hours by the time Andrew finally showed up. He had been called by the house, and when he got there, he shoved everyone out of my room.

As he closed the door, I sat up in bed.

"What are you doing here?" I asked, slurring my words. He understood what was wrong. He knew, somehow, this was because he had not shown up.

"What the fuck did you do?" he asked while propping my head up.

"I just wanted to go to sleep," I said. He knew about my sleeping pill habit and disapproved when it resurfaced from time to time.

He started crying. I may have been incoherent, half-baked on sleeping pills, and not really in my right mind, but I remember staring into his face and seeing tears streaming down it as he genuinely feared what he thought I might have been trying to do. We were both depressed; we knew what that might mean in a world of what felt like very limited means of escape, even if neither of us had never directly used the word "suicide."

"Don't you ever fucking..." he said, his sentence trailing off. Then he leaned in and kissed me on the cheek.

I had never felt such love, such value, and it became seared into my brain for all eternity. I remember every inch of his face, every pimple, every lash surrounding his deep brown eyes, every strand of his shaggy brown hair. Someone actually cared whether I lived or died. He had actually kissed me—yeah, on the cheek, but had I turned my face just enough, I have no doubt he would have kissed me on the mouth. I think both of us were scared by what we knew existed just below the surface. So that didn't happen. He slept in my bed that night, pressed up against me, partly to monitor me and partly to comfort me.

A few weeks later, Andrew had his own emotional episode, and then I became the caretaker. In this instance, he was more intoxicated than I'd ever seen him, to the point where I wondered if, even if it violated the unofficial house rules, I should call 911. He had spent the night being taunted by some brothers over our "too-close" friendship but still ended up back in what had become, for all intents and purposes, our room. He was very depressed, and he was crying, worrying he would end up alone. After a night of being forced to focus on what "we" were, he drank himself into a stupor worrying what being gay or bisexual meant and if it had destroyed any chance of happiness. I knew the feeling; I'd wept for that same reason. This time I kissed him on the cheek. This time, he attempted a return kiss on the lips, but I turned away, embarrassed and unsure of what this would mean with him in such a vulnerable position. I was concerned with him being faced with a decision that could send him over the edge. I knew what had happened with James—hell, even to me. I slept on the couch that night.

That evening bookended our mutual crises and foreshadowed where things were headed. It was now spring, and instead of a new relationship coming out of our emotional entanglement, it was headed towards collapse. Neither of us was ready to be truly honest about "us," even if we had been transparently open about our individual selves in every other way. Even then, I knew was not a good idea for two sexually confused people to embrace the intensely fraught nature of a friendship turned romantic in the midst of depression, poverty, loneliness, and fear. It's an even worse idea among fellow fraternity brothers who have been trained in the cruelty of social ostracization in ways that would make one blush. So, when my nemesis Omid re-entered my life in a few short weeks, there was no Andrew to fall back on, no house to protect me. And bereft of the only love I had known, Omid's cruelty and revenge would send me off the deep end.

CHAPTER 10

THE COLLAPSE—TAKE II

A few months after Andrew's and my not-so-innocent pecks on the cheeks, a series of destabilizing events yanked my entire world out from under me. I was left forlorn, lost, and gazing at the bottom of the proverbial barrel during the spring of my senior year. In this case, it was an actual rain barrel outside the Strawberry Creek Inn, a bed and breakfast I had escaped to in the mountains outside Los Angeles. Idyllwild, the town I was temporarily calling home, was in a drought, and it was common to find buildings like this one collecting rainwater. It's funny how literal some of life's moments can be, but at that moment, I didn't find any of it amusing.

I stood there, my reflection staring at me from the water, not liking what I saw. Narcissus in reverse. I could have stood for hours, and no one would have stopped me. No one knew me, and Lori, Andrew's Lori who sent me there, had contacted the bed and breakfast's owners in advance, telling them I needed space. I had nowhere else to be. As I fled Los Angeles the night before, I hastily emailed anyone who might be reasonably expected to wonder where I was (though I doubted they would) that I had to leave and I did not know when I'd be back. No one emailed back with any concerns, sadly. Either they didn't want to know what was happening or they didn't care. The only response I got was from my job saying, "Let us know when you're back."

So there I was on a frigid early morning in the mountains, staring into a barrel of rainwater, realizing this was my lowest point. For all the past cookies, boots, and Christmases, this moment stood out more than any other as the crowning achievement of my failure to make a life that I thought was like everyone else's in some small way. Time and time again, I thought I had found an opportunity, only to realize I was chasing a phantom, like a reflection on the water that disappears when you brush your hand across it.

With every failure, the pain went deeper, and the next opportunity was even more heightened and riskier, as if my chances were running out. My life had become a series of moments of finding myself in new places with more stress, more fear, and less time. As the sun came up that morning and I stared at the ceiling of my temporary bedroom, my mental catalog of ceilings gained another addition before I dragged myself out of bed and walked to this point standing over the rain barrel.

I had nowhere to go, no one to see, and nothing to do but sit with my own thoughts. The situation was absolutely terrifying, confounding, and completely pointless. I hated being alone, but now it was my only option, at least until I figured out what to do next.

I took a few moments to examine the town around me. The stores were still closed. I had not eaten that morning, but I was so wired from anxiety I wasn't hungry. So, I decided I'd go for a walk or a hike, even. I had never been on a hike, and I didn't really know what one was. I knew that people went to Malibu or Runyon Canyon to "hike," but I hadn't ever done it. I figured that this day it would be whatever I wanted it to be. I set off toward the meadows and forests around the town, not following any path, with no destination, no guide, and no way of reaching the outside world.

I wandered through the trees, climbing slowly upward. The path was gentle, and the forest was starting to bloom as winter ebbed and the trees realized it was time to come back to life after a long winter. I wished I could feel the same in that moment. I wasn't sure if I'd ever feel any sense of joy again—that's what the combination of a first heartbreak combined with the complete collapse of your life can do to you, I had discovered. As bad as DePauw had been, suddenly it seemed so much "less than" by being only one of those two tracks of loss.

The first loss was Andrew. It started just after his drunken kiss on the cheek. It turns out, his feelings that night may have been brought out by alcohol, but they were the latest iteration of terrifying emotions he didn't want to feel. Like me, he wanted to feel normal and be normal. That meant not loving me, and he began distancing himself from me.

It started little by little, as he made new friends who I kept mocking as superficial. William, his tall and lanky current object of attention, was rich enough he never bothered to fix his hair or put any effort in his appearance. Being lazy was an affectation of privilege. Growing up poor, I had consistently done the opposite to mask my background, so I guess we both had a bit of a "tell," and I resented him for his. Will's girlfriend, whose generic name is lost to my memory, had a friend Andrew had become romantically interested in, though he denied it. Tess was her name, and it was clear to me he was attracted to her, if only because she had a Porsche and her dad had an Oscar he let Andrew hold.

But Tess was also the kind of girl who said stupid shit without thinking, and that really annoyed me. When hanging out with all of them at a museum one afternoon, I heard her yammer as she stood staring at Van Gogh's last painting and wondered aloud, "Oh my god, it's just like you can see he was crazy. It's all so random." I nearly slapped her into the previous Tuesday. Art critic extraordinaire she was not, and I was offended at her blatant misunderstanding of mental illness, one Andrew and I both suffered from. I spent the rest of the day using what wit I had to pick apart every fallacy, boast, and cliche that dropped out of her mouth. That day ended predictably, with Andrew yelling at me in my room, or what had become our room. How dare I be mean to her? How dare I embarrass him? My protests of her insipidness fell on deaf ears.

It wasn't just Tess, Generic Girl, and William. Andrew began to hang out with more bros in the house, the ones he had spent months privately lambasting. He began smoking weed, a habit I detested. He slept over less and less, and little by little, our relationship, whatever it was, fell apart. Any time I pleaded with him for honesty, out of fear, worry, or just sadness, he would say he still loved me and we were still "in it together." He had begun using the word love, with a nominal platonic cover, in that way one might when covering one's true intentions. Every time you cheat, you call home more. Every time you stray, you reaffirm your affections. It's almost an inverse ratio correlated to every Lifetime movie ever made.

The final straw was my birthday. I had stopped celebrating it years ago, just before the parents disowned me. I was turning twelve, planning a birthday with my twin sister, when I was suddenly informed I was not invited. There would still be a birthday, but she had grown tired of sharing it with me. So, our aunts and uncles and cousins and her friends would be invited, but I was expected to stay in my room in the basement. It seemed, to me at the time, an expected bit of cruelty. I didn't protest; I had long since stopped crying. I certainly never had my own party, and because of that incident, I refused to acknowledge I even had a birthday. Ten years later, I had confessed to Andrew, and only Andrew, how that had felt. He had planned a special night for my birthday: dinner and a trip to the Opera. He was dead set on resurrecting my long-dead celebration.

Naively, I thought maybe it would build a bridge between us, maybe a fresh start. He didn't show up. It was like being punched in the face. I had chosen to share one of my most vulnerable moments with him, the day it was made clear I shouldn't have been born and how important it was to me. I was crushed.

My defeat at Andrew's hands was only part of the reason I was in the mountains running away from life. As I marched through the forests of Idyllwild, I realized I had the unique ability to create perfect life storms. I came across a creek cascading down through a grove of trees and piles of large, broken rocks. They were jagged and precarious in places, safe in others. I decided to climb up the rockface. This was as good a time as any to try climbing them, no point or purpose in sight other than testing the grip of my bare hands and sneakers in this rugged landscape.

My hands hurt as I pulled myself up the stones. My palms still bore the scars of my latest coping mechanism. I had begun cutting myself with a serrated butter knife. As Andrew's and my relationship had deteriorated, I turned not just to increasing amounts of sleeping pills but also to sitting quietly in my room, caressing the skin on the inside of my hand with a dull blade. I had no desire to cut a major artery; I just wanted to feel something. The rough, barely serrated edge gave me moments to contemplate. I never cut too deep—just enough to see a small gash that would heal in a few days.

It seemed at times like those cuts relieved not just the pressure of losing Andrew but also the fraternity. That was the second track of my loss. While Andrew carved out my heart by distancing himself, the house gutted my reality by taking away a place to live, food, and my future. It started slowly at first.

For starters, part of my protective shield had failed. I had been forced into being an emeritus social chair and had to train my replacements as I headed out the door to graduation, which meant two younger bros were now in charge. I grew more distant from the house, and I floated with unknown value. Omid resurfaced. He had been lying in wait to strike like Scar from *The Lion King*, hoping to find the right moment. He had tagged my black Ford Explorer with the word "faggot" in soap, one of the only times I've ever been subjected to a slur of that type. When he taunted me in the hallways, knocking books out of my hands and threatening me, it was like being transported back to high school. When no one was looking, he would barge into my room and tell me he was going to hurt me. Like the abusive husband or bro that he was, he would alternate between these threats with intoxicated bouts of vulnerability, asking why I didn't like him or why I refused to "bond" with the rest of the house like he had.

As I climbed the last of the rocks to the top of the tiny waterfall of cold mountain snow melt, I sat there remembering how the last part of my world had fallen apart. If this was hiking, it wasn't strenuous, but it was quiet enough that I could stare at the sky for hours and let memories sink in. I couldn't hear the shouts of the bros accusing me of bringing disrepute and damage to the house for going public about Omid's threats.

When I had asked for action to curb Omid's increasingly frequent and terrifying attacks, they tried to minimize his behavior. They would tell me "He was just drunk" or "He wouldn't *really* do anything."

I went along with them until it was suddenly clear he could do something devastating the day he attacked me, brick in hand. While I was hiking, I picked up a rock as I made my way through the forest. Omid's brick had been about the same size. It was being used as a doorstop at the back door outside my room. When Omid found out I asked the house to step in because of his threatening behavior, he confronted me one sunny afternoon outside my room. The door was propped open, and I moved toward my usual quick escape, but he blocked my way. He screamed obscenities in my face in only the way a guilty person or a *Real Housewife* can. He pushed me, but I didn't fight back. I knew he wanted a fight; it would give him license to do more injury, and I was not about to do that. My reticence angered him even more, and he pushed me to the ground. He knelt on top of me, claiming I liked it "rough," and spit in my face. I tried to get away, but Omid had put on the "freshman twenty" every year since freshman year, so that was not a viable exit strategy. I was going to have to wait this out until help came. It would pass, I told myself, and I believed it until Omid picked up the brick propping the back door open and held it above my head.

The veins in his neck were popping as he kept me down with one hand and took terrifying joy in threating to bash in my "little faggot head." By this point, his taunts and my cries for help had become loud enough that a few bros had gathered to watch. That's what happens in fraternities: you watch the fight and regret your lack of action later, if at all. One of them had the minimal presence of mind to get the newly elected president, Peter, who came running. Peter was the one who said Omid was not dangerous, but now he was pulling a grown man off me who was holding a brick capable of crushing my skull.

As Peter focused on pulling Omid off me and calming him down, it struck me our dear president was more concerned with his reputation and this psychopath's mental state than with my current near-death situation. As Peter and Omid turned the corner to leave, I saw Andrew. He had been standing there for some time, watching this man threaten my life. We had become distant enough he either felt no compunction to help me, or he knew that doing so would expose him to further abuse from the house because of our relationship. I was furious, hurt, and desperate for revenge on someone, anyone.

I found Peter and demanded action. He demurred again. It wasn't serious, he said. It felt serious to me, I insisted. "Do something!" I demanded, or I would. Peter warned me to be patient and not to do anything to anger the house. I was already in hot water with many there who had not liked the changes I had made. "What, more success and more preppiness?" I asked. Peter nodded. The conversation did not end well.

I knew Peter was right. Nothing would happen to Omid inside the house, and if I went outside the house, I would be in trouble. One didn't go outside the house with problems. But I feared for my safety, and that fear combined with a desire to hurt someone, anyone, brought me to a bad place. Since I could not do anything about Andrew, I could at least get Omid, and he deserved whatever punishment befell him. I went to the administration to file a formal complaint, and the house went batshit nuts. I had already been on thin ice. Now absent the protections of being social chair, they attacked me full tilt, claiming I had turned on them first.

My formal complaint would trigger a school investigation, we all knew, and with investigations came interviews, reports, and an examination of everything in the fraternity. Turn any corner and you'd find a number of legal and University violations: casual drug use, underage drinking, violent physical hazing, all the things that make American students into the leaders of tomorrow. The fear was that the University would turn over every rock to find any problem they could and close the fraternity in the process. I had endangered the house, and I had done so willfully and wantonly to hurt Omid, to hurt Andrew, and to shed what once had value but was now empty to me.

When the news broke, the house membership was summoned for a general meeting. I was nominally expelled and given a month to move out. The decision was ludicrous; there were only two months left in the semester, and most members knew it was a joke. However, a strong and furious assault on my character combined with a desire to make an example of me and a herd mentality forced a close but losing vote for me. My social chair protégé Alex vowed he would work back channels to reverse the decision, but I was bereft of hope. The second of my two tracks of loss was complete: I was without someone to love and without a place to live. Once again, I felt like I was back at zero and would have to start over.

Sure, I thought, walking through the trees weeks later as I plucked fresh leaves from branches, these guys were not my friends. But they were all I had left. Like being a part of the mafia, they were the closest thing to family I had. They also meant stability, housing, food—my life depended on what the fraternity provided, and I did not have the money for a new apartment. How would I manage finals? Would I be able to hold on to the few connections of this little world I had built? How would I even graduate? This time there was no kind lady from financial aid providing a soft landing; the house had dealt a blow out of nowhere, and the end was here. I retreated to my room, but then the drop-ins started. Bros were coming to console or gloat, and I simply couldn't take any of it. I needed to go.

I had lost Andrew, who had gone from soulmate to spectator, watching me have my head nearly bashed in. I had lost my social status, going from social chair to pariah. No matter how manufactured and fake, manufactured and fake were the stock and trade of USC. Is it any wonder, then, that my body followed suit when the world came crashing down? Alone in my room, I had a panic attack, crying and gasping violently for breath. I was scared, and I didn't know where to turn. I ran out the back door and down the street in flip flops, a cheap pair of shorts, and a t-shirt. Mindlessly running, I ended up at the door of a sorority where Emily, an acquaintance of mine, lived. I was frantically pounding on the door of Alpha Delta Pi, and even though she and I were not that close, that night, she was the person I turned to. I kept banging on the door and demanded to see her.

Boys are not allowed into the residential parts of sorority houses, but when they opened their door and saw I was clearly in such a terrible state, no one objected. I collapsed on the floor of Emily's room, sobbing and heaving, barely able to form words. In a moment of desperation, hoping for any comfort, I looked up and saw her eyes. They were sympathetic but distant. This young woman had suddenly had a "half-friend" show up on her doorstep appearing nearly insane, who then collapsed on her bedroom floor. I came to and felt empty and embarrassed. I got up and ran out of the room without a word, down the stairs, and out the back door. Emily chased behind, as did a few other girls, but after hopping over a hedge or two, I was beyond their reach and long gone into the darker crevasses of USC's main campus.

Standing in Idyllwild a few days later, recalling that memory, I was unconsciously ripping leaves into tiny pieces. Then I realized had no idea where I was. I stopped to look around. I might have been gone hours—I wasn't sure at this point—but the sun was high in the sky, and I was definitely lost. This was strange and familiar all at once. I had nowhere to be, I thought to myself, and so I headed in a random direction. The only way back was down, which seemed oddly appropriate. I continued my meandering path. Best-case scenario, I'd be eaten by a pack of wolves.

The wolves were after me that night back at USC, as well. I sat by a secret little fountain I knew in an out-of-the-way spot near a building called Town and Gown. I listened to the water trickle down as I tried to compose myself. I had lost Andrew, I had lost the house, I had lost any friends I had, and I had unequivocally embarrassed myself in the process. That last one seemed to be the deepest cut of all.

Ever since I had fled thirteen years prior with a plate of cookies, I had vowed to find an escape. No matter how poor I was, how clueless in manners or social mores, I had studied them and abided by them. I tried to dress the part, much to my credit card's discomfort. I carried myself confidently in class. I became expert at listening to the start of a conversation and then regurgitating what I had heard with just enough twist to sound original. I wanted to fit in, I had to fit in, and I became well practiced at mimicry. It had started back at DePauw with Kevin, and I had gotten better since.

But in one night, at my wit's end, all that work, all that preparation, all that effort just vanished. I had broken down in front of everyone and lost it all. As if my sleeping pill incident a few months earlier was not enough, this time I was entirely conscious and desperately trying to catch my breath. My reputational façade was revealed to be a sham, a complete disaster. The fountain at USC didn't seem to care, nor did the rocks and trees around me in Idyllwild. Here in the mountains, all the stones seemed freeing in their expansiveness, as if equally indifferent to my plight.

The complete and total breakdown of a previously calm grade A student was enough to worry both the girls of Alpha Delta Pi and surprisingly, even, some of the bros at my house, so they sent search parties out. I did not realize it at first, since no one *ever* called the authorities at USC, but suddenly I noticed there was a larger than usual number of University Public Safety officers around. I dodged and weaved to avoid detection. Maybe I was being paranoid, but I had heard stories about how private universities could send you to the hospital for almost anything they wanted or even expel you. Having lost almost everything, the last thing I had left to lose was my degree, as well. As I threaded my way towards Hoover Street to head back to what I had left of my home, I was finally composed enough to slip in unnoticed, or so I thought. A patrol car pulled up alongside me. The officers played it cool.

"You need a ride?" they asked.

"No, I'm good," I responded calmly.

"Are you sure?" they insisted, their tone almost pleading.

"Yep, I'm almost home."

The car continued to roll slowly next to me as they assessed the situation. I would find out later they had been told I was on the verge of a breakdown or an even more serious incident, and perhaps I was. But the kid they now saw seemed fine. Something wasn't adding up, but they couldn't take action without some sort of provocation.

"You wouldn't happen to be Craig, would you?"

"Yeah," I responded, stopping to face the music. "Can I help you?"

The officer looked at me. I realized in that moment just how young he was, barely old enough to have graduated himself. I saw sympathy in his face, but I didn't trust him any more than Omid.

"Listen," he said. "There are a lot of people worried about you. So, you know…" He paused, not sure how far to go. "If I had people worried about me, I'd want them to know I was all right. Why don't you let me give you a ride?"

"I'm good," I said. "I'm just three blocks away, and I'll be home soon. They know I'm fine."

I turned on my heels and walked away. The car lingered a bit longer and then pulled away. I was in the clear, narrowly avoiding some sort of mental evaluation, which I probably had only a fifty-fifty chance of passing. I was, in fact, in a precarious position at the moment. The scars on my palms, the empty bottles of sleeping pills, and the public breakdowns didn't paint the prettiest picture. It was the one and only time I had come close to thinking about, plotting, and seriously planning suicide, but I was sufficiently deterred by Pascal's Bet. If there was a hell, my Catholic upbringing made it clear I'd be fucked. That was enough to give me pause while I figured out if the knife should cut a bit deeper into my palm next time. I had to think, and I had to get out of dodge.

I called Lori immediately. She and I had grown closer, and I had called her in times of need over the past few months. It was late in her time zone, but she picked up anyway. Saint that she was, she always picked up. She reassured me that Andrew still loved me even if he couldn't express it, but she also encouraged me to find my own way. I needed to leave LA, I said, but I did not know where to go.

"Don't worry, I'll take care of it," she said. "Give me an hour, pack a bag, and get in your car and then call me. I'll tell you where to go."

Slipping in and out of the house unnoticed through my escape hatch, that's exactly what I did, and two hours later, I checked into the blessed Strawberry Inn. Twelve hours later, I had washed my tear-stained face and marched up this goddamn hill in the middle of nowhere. After having climbed a few dozen large rocks, stuck my hand in a frigid waterfall, and torn apart approximately 573 leaves piece by piece, I wound my way down out of the clouds. Somehow, I found myself back in civilization.

I came across a road and then suddenly wasn't lost anymore. Idyllwild was a mile east, and I was back on a route I knew. As I walked into town, shops were now open, and people were milling about. I wandered through stores filled with things I didn't want or need, and when that ran its course, I spent the rest of the evening reading and crying.

The next morning, I went down to breakfast, something that shocked the owners of the inn, who had been assured I wanted to be alone. I was by myself at the table as they served me toast and eggs until a Japanese woman sat down beside me.

I looked a fright, I'm sure. I came to find out that she was a caring mom. Being emotionally intuitive, she did not ask about my situation. She did, however, cleverly share her own story in a way I'm sure she hoped would provide some clarity to a confused-looking young man. I don't remember her name, but to this day, I am grateful for what she said.

Miss A., I'll call her, revealed she lived in Japan, in a culture where people weren't allowed to express themselves. She had been a flautist but was now a functionary in finance, a low-level bookkeeper working ninety hours a week just to make ends meet. She hated her life, but it was worth it because of her daughter, a young girl who was not at the table. When I inquired as to her whereabouts, Miss A. reveled her daughter was at a weeklong music camp in Idyllwild and being considered for admission to an arts school. Miss A. had noticed early that her daughter had a penchant for music like her mother. And unlike her own father, Miss A. had taken every difficult step to allow her daughter to express herself and pursue her passion, even if it meant giving up any personal time by taking an extra shift at work to pay for more lessons.

"I just know, I know what I grew up with, where dreams are crushed. You are told you have to be like everyone else.

You are told this, this is what we do," Miss A. said. "And I don't want her to go through that. I don't want her to be like everyone else. I want my daughter to be herself. I want her to leave me, leave Japan, and go to school in the United States. I want her to realize to be like everyone else will kill your soul. That is why I bring her here," she finished in broken English.

I nearly burst out crying. Miss A. was caringly telling me the one piece of advice I had never heard. It wasn't out of admonition, as it had been from Mrs. Cash or Joe. It wasn't out of self-interest, as it was for my professorial mentors. It was simply out of love, her love for her daughter and love for a life she herself had given up. All I had wanted was normalcy, thinking it would bring me even just one authentic human connection from James, from Andrew, from anyone, and yet Miss A. was convinced happiness, including the passions of expression and authentic human connection, lay down a different road entirely. They lay inside oneself, not with others.

I realized on another hike later that day, my second of many that week, a real connection was not possible for me at the moment. But, I thought, maybe I did not have to be normal to find one after all. I had spent my entire life, not just my adult life but my entire waking life, trying to be someone other people wanted. My parents had not wanted me, but maybe someone else would, provided I looked and acted like all the kids, teenagers, and adults I saw on television and in magazines. If I chased it hard enough, if I were smart enough, adult enough, stylish enough, educated enough, popular enough, if I were anything, then I might be enough.

Now suddenly, Miss A. helped me realize there were some people who were themselves, and that was enough for them. Normalcy didn't have anything to do with it—finding yourself did. I didn't yet know if that could be me. One cannot just undo over a decade of bad choices and self-induced propaganda in a moment. But a week by myself in the mountains, staring hard at the bottom of the barrel that was my life…it would get me started on that journey.

Change in the coming weeks was rough going. My twin losses loomed large upon my return to USC. The split with Andrew was still awful, and I carried incredible anger, though I learned to bottle it dangerously deep inside. On the other hand, Alex kept his word and got the house to reverse my expulsion because I kept my mouth shut and withdrew my complaint, hard enough in the abstract but even more so in practice.

I graduated in a few weeks, and Lori flew out to celebrate with the fanciest dinner she could arrange. I didn't feel like much celebrating, but she insisted this was a moment to commemorate, even if I didn't think so. I think I threw up twice at dinner and cried in the bathroom, distraught, anxious and filled with loss. Even though Miss A. had helped me see something through the gloom, a path up from my pit of despair, any progress would still be in halting fits and starts. As I started my post-college career, life would not get any easier or better, and I didn't seem to care. I just played the part.

I had not gained the tools necessary to grow; I had only been given the information necessary to accept and compartmentalize.

Life immediately after college was simple in its own way. I found a job working at a movie studio. Show up, do the work, get paid. I signed up for every hour of overtime I could find and found myself at work from seven a.m. to two a.m. almost every day. When you're crushed at work, it's easy to ignore the rest of your life. What little free time I did have, I spent in the pool, swimming for hours on end, trying to recreate the silence and peace of Idyllwild. At least underwater or out in a club with throbbing music, I could drown out the world around me. I was, to the outside world, a normal twenty-two-year-old in his first job. Running from office to red carpet to fetching coffee, I was, in reality, just a shadow of a human being, slowly unwinding years of conditioning thanks to Miss A.'s transformative talk. But it was a slow process. Pain is not easy to undo or to let go of.

I had one mark of progress now, though; in time, perhaps, more would come. For the first time in my life, as college ended and the rest of my life began, I realized I could accept not being normal. That could be enough, a simple step forward. I could stop chasing it like a gold medal at the end of some unending race. The only problem is, when you've been searching for something your entire life and you stop, what the hell do you do next? One step at a time, life was about to show me how to find my way back up, just as it had shown me how to slide down.

PART II:
THE WAY UP

CHAPTER 11

A NEW MOM

For me, graduating from college wasn't like the hopeful starts you see in greeting cards and holiday movies. Finally, I had a fresh start that wasn't the result of being abandoned, discarded, or forced. It should have been a banner moment, but it wasn't. I had realized I didn't have to chase something I wasn't, but I had no idea who I was. I was still, after twenty-two years, alone. If there was one thing I knew, however, it was how to function in life while still being lost and alone.

First and foremost, I knew I had to find a way to stay in Los Angeles. Outside the bubble of USC, I was more on my own than ever, and the previous Christmas had ensured that if I returned to the Midwest, it was going to be in a pine box, not voluntarily. Thankfully, I had worked my ass off throughout college and charted the path to a full-time job in Hollywood, even as I circled the drain emotionally. I worked for famous film studios, first doing grunt work but then being pulled into far more. It turns out if your boss discovers that you can do part of his or her job for them and you're willing to take the lower paycheck and no credit, you get more interesting work. So it was, running from press junkets to press tours to premieres, all in marketing and publicity for films. And if there was a problem? I solved it. A nightmare film, an impossible marketing request, a terrifying political situation? The same traits that had helped me survive until this point, being able to read people and tenaciously pursuing the goals I assigned myself, made me indispensable. To others, it might have been a life; to me, it was just work and money, serving a utilitarian end to survive, as it always had.

Socially, I had no opportunity for escape behind a desk or on a red carpet, which meant turning to other diversions. Giving up a decade of pretending, hoping, praying, and crying was not an overnight assignment. So, I burned the candle at both ends, staying out late partying after work and getting home just in time to start the day over again. I found myself running with the "gay mafia" in Los Angeles, a cabal of gay men casting films via sexual favors, hosting house parties that ran until dawn. I figured if I was going to do the gay thing, I should at least get to have a good time. I numbed myself with things like sex with a DJ in a club and had random encounters in bathrooms. I held crushes and real dating at arm's length, and it was the same for real friendships. At work, I was a distant figure, an assistant who got shit done but never talked about anything that wasn't work related. I would later come to learn people viewed me as unfriendly. No matter. My competency saved me, as it had as social chair.

In the end, however, behind the clubs, the sex, and the eighteen-hour workdays, I was still almost violently alone.

I had no pride, no joy, no redemption. I felt like I was watching the world through soundproof glass, and everyone else on the other side had purpose, meaning, and comfort. It was all just a blunt, banal experience, pretending everything was good, when I was really treading water aimlessly. What was my goal if no longer to pretend to be like everyone else? What was my purpose?

My saving grace and the foundation of my baby steps out of my darkness would come from a something I'd never expected: parents. Not "the original" parents, of course. My ties had long been cut there. *Those* parents were now gone, and a new pair would now unexpectedly present themselves.

Bear with me. I'd previously considered the people I grew up with as my parents, as biological parents, discovering years later even that was not true. Sadly, I'd never know who my actual parents were, so my "parents" in Indiana now became re-labeled as "the originals." They were just a set of people I grew up around and called by their first names, Dale and Joan. Now, after college, two people would emerge to replace them.

In this early version of my new life, I found myself on the receiving end of a completely different situation: two new parents who hadn't given birth to me, hadn't raised me, and hadn't known me until just a few years earlier. I'd finally find people who would truly be *my* parents, by choice, by right, and by love. My new parents, going forward, were two unbelievable people named Rob and Kathy. Of course, like all things in my life, this development was circuitous in nature.

It had started in college. While the rest of the fraternity had largely retreated from me during *la Grande Scandale*, a few brothers had stayed in my orbit, including one named Robbie. He was awkward, endearingly peculiar, and anti-social, but there was an authenticity to him. And over time, his awkwardness would blossom into a singular genuineness. His shyness would turn into attachment, and after college he and I would start hanging out as something resembling actual friends.

Spending time together was a comfort. I had someone to hang out with and experience life with but who demanded almost no emotional commitment or openness. He did not share much, and I shared less. His emotional immaturity was a nice match for my unwillingness to discuss my complete and total wreck of a life. Through our time together, we developed an unlikely and unexpected bond. Most importantly, he introduced me to his family, a Norman-Rockwell-inspired example of San Marino, California perfection. His parents, Rob and Kathy, were still head over heels in love after thirty years of marriage and had two daughters who exceled at their work and were best friends. Their son, Robbie, loved them all deeply and they him. It was a concept new to me up close.

The only time I ever saw Robbie's family fight was over not spending enough time together. Their friendliness and generosity was foreign to me, but it was the balm of Gilead. Every time I went to their house, I was invited for dinner. Rob and Kathy, the parents, inquired about my life with actual concern. They genuinely cared, and suddenly, I found myself, bit by bit, in an unfamiliar situation: among people who didn't want anything from me, who did not care if

I could read a room, and who simply wondered what wine I wanted from their abundantly stocked cellar. Shortly after I graduated, they moved just a mile away from me, and I spent more and more time with them, even when Robbie was not around.

At first, it was an unsettling and new experience for me to spend time with people that wasn't transactional in some way. Rob and Kathy were good parents, and they cared about their children. They shared things with me. They listened to me when I shared things with them, and they didn't push more than I was willing to give. They treated me as if I were a family member, moving beyond general conversation, veering into unsolicited advice. If the latter is not parenting, I don't know what is.

Throughout, it was as if I was living in the Twilight Zone. I was not in any family photos, but I was included in holidays. I wasn't close to the daughters, but Robbie was the only friend I had. Where was I in all of this? Who were these people, and why was I in this weird half in, half out situation? I didn't know, and in my tetherless state, I was not particularly inclined to ask. Even half in was more than I had ever had. My time with them was a welcome respite, even if it was an imperfect one that also left me confused.

Then, one day, Kathy asked if I would go shopping with her. The family was getting ready for a Christmas ski trip, a mostly annual ritual in their own world of storybook perfection. I had nothing better to do, and she said she wanted my advice on a new outfit while none of her children were around to help. I went, of course, as I never turned down an invitation from Rob or Kathy. In the gray routine of my life, they were the "sometime spice," a break in the monotony of rolling calls, drinking with strangers all night, and lying to the press about a celebrity's personal life.

I met up with Kathy at the sporting goods store across from the Beverly Center, an unintended memorial to concrete and steel that stood out like a sore thumb in the middle of Los Angeles. A fancier, nicer, and more enticing mall had opened down the street, but the Beverly Center remained like a fortress over the passage of time. The Beverly Center was terminally in 1996 and so was the adjacent Beverly Connection, a smaller complex that might have well as contained a Radio Shack. Beverly Connection's only bright spots were Ross Dress for Less, a discount clothing store, and Sports Chalet, where you could get anything you needed, from Runyon Canyon Lululemon to, as I would discover, ski equipment. This is where we met that day.

I had stopped reading the room with Kathy and Rob and the family because there never seemed to be much to read that wasn't already apparent. There was no superficiality and no pretense. Plus, Kathy was terrible at keeping secrets. If you wanted to make sure the family knew something, you told her. So that day as we wandered around the store, I didn't think anything of it when she said it was no fun trying on new ski clothes alone and I should grab some. I was blithely unaware of what was actually happening, and she was cutesy like that. I always liked new clothes and indulged by trying on garments I could never afford. I would stare in the mirror and imagine being able to buy something as nice. At the time, my wardrobe still came from the Express Men's clearance sale specials and leftover luxury event gift bags. So that day, I happily went along for the ride just for the fun of it.

Kathy donned a bright pink suit with matching jacket—"something bright" to see her going down the mountain, she said. I tried on many different patterns and outfits, not well-chosen and all far more adventurous fashion choices. Never one to hide her opinion, she expressed her clear dislike for anything too outrageous. I knew that my choices were amateurish and garish, so I humored her until I found an outfit she and I agreed on and then put it all away. As I dressed, she told me to meet her at the exit. She had her outfit, and it was time to head home for a glass of red wine "with Papa," as she lovingly called her husband.

When I got out of the fitting room, I headed to meet up with her to leave. She wasn't at the exit, though. I found her still at the check-out, credit card in hand. She had her outfit but also the one I had tried on, both being put in a big shopping bag. It may sound unbelievable, but I never thought she would buy the clothes for me. I didn't even need them; I didn't ski and had no plans to. I was deeply uncomfortable with gifts or when anyone spent money on me. I protested, especially over something I would never need.

"You don't have to do that, I don't need them," I protested. "And it's too expensive." It was more expensive than anything I owned.

"Don't be ridiculous," she said matter-of-factly. She wasn't being coy; she was serious. She relished doing nice things, and this was just one of them. "You're going to need it for the trip."

"What trip?" I asked, even though I knew what she was talking about. They had been talking for weeks about the annual ski trip, and I had never thought I'd be invited, no matter how much time we all spent together. I winced a little whenever they mentioned it. I forced myself to remember that no matter how wonderful it felt to spend time with them, they were not my family, and so I didn't expect to be fully integrated into their lives.

"Don't be silly. We're going to Mammoth for Christmas, and you can't wear jeans. You need something to ski in. Papa and everyone else will be going down the black diamond trails, but you can be with me on the lower runs." She remembered my fear of heights and was going to make a special effort to spend time with me on the slopes.

For a second time, Christmas played a significant role in my understanding what it meant to be human and connect to other people. Once on the trip, it was not just about a vacation, a Christmas turkey, or watching the intimacy of Kelley and Kristen fighting in front of everyone, frustrations unfiltered to those around because they were "family." No, more than anything, it was about the day Kathy pulled my hair.

On the second day of the trip, Robbie and I went out in the worst blizzard in a decade to check on my car, which was under seven feet of snow. Mission accomplished, we decided to explore. We had a great time wandering across the mountain, jumping into drifts, and climbing out by packing snow carefully into small steps. When the storm picked up even more, we started back to the cabin. Hours had passed blissfully in the white-out conditions as Robbie and I joked around, laughing harder than I ever had. We were as carefree as two people could be. I remember thinking, this is what youth must be like.

As we returned to the cabin, though, it was clear something had gone sideways. There were patrol lights flashing on a snowmobile outside the cabin, and when we entered, Kathy was livid. She always maintained an unflappable exterior, but she was more upset than I had ever seen. She ripped the hat off my head and grabbed my hair in her fist, yanking my face within inches of hers, all five-foot-two against my six-foot-one advantage. She did the same to Robbie, but he got away from her, while I stood in terror. Her face was furious, and I saw true vulnerability and fear in her eyes.

"How dare you!" she said, her voice filled with a weird kind of rage I had never seen. It was crushing yet soft at the same time. She yelled at me that we had left without phones, said we'd be gone minutes, and yet here we were, missing hours later. Crews had been looking for us in what were truly dangerous weather conditions. To Robbie and me, it had been harmless fun. To his parents, it was an unexpected, dangerous situation.

"Don't you ever do that again!" she commanded with rage. "You could have been lost! You could have died!"

She was hurt. She was fearful. She was honest and open. All I could offer was a blank stare. I stood speechless, trying to process why she was so upset. No one had ever been angry with me like this. Still, once I realized what was happening, oddly it was one of the happiest moments I had ever experienced. Of course, I was incredibly sorry to have scared and hurt her, but I was quietly welling up with a new feeling: value.

I had been important to Joan because I satisfied her need to be loved, important to bros for the parties I threw, important at work for the answers I provided. My life was about what I gave others. With Kathy and Rob, however, it seemed I just took and took, and they gave. Now here I was, soaking wet from melting snow, hair clenched in a lady's fist, being screamed at for scaring her, and I realized I had never been cared about so much in my life. I burst into tears, and she relented, letting go.

She probably thought it was because I was sad; she did not know she had tapped something else inside me. I was nine all over again, except this time my parents had worried about me running away; I was seventeen, and my teacher cared about my lonely mornings in the library; I was nineteen, and my professors cared about my sanity as I faced expulsion; I was twenty-one, and my fraternity did not want to see a brick smacked into my head. It was the opposite of my prior reality. If there was any time my expected reality had been flipped on its head, it was this moment. Kathy's passion and care did not fix any of my past, but it was the first step forward I had taken since Idyllwild. My tears were simply an acknowledgement of that.

I looked over at Robbie to see if he realized what was going on—if he too felt value from such an experience. No, this was not new to him. He had grown up with people caring what happened to him—it was normal and merited no extra attention. Having to wrest himself away from his mother's grip on his hair was normal to him, while to me it was unfathomable. Through no fault of his own, he couldn't know how profound it was simply having a parent show concern for your well-being.

That Christmas trip ended without further incident. As I returned to Los Angeles with the family, things seemed to return to their usual gray area. It was still confusing to be left out at times while included in others, but I knew in the midst of it all, if I died, someone might actually show up to my funeral. That little idea began to grow deep at the bottom of the ocean of my consciousness, eventually becoming something I would be able to float on.

While the relationship with my new quasi-parents was a profound change, I was still struggling to turn the corner. The occasional break at their home couldn't outweigh the other 120 hours a week I wasn't there. I was still feeling adrift and lost. Two years after college, I was meandering through life, purposeless and in pain from the last assault on my heart at USC. I needed to find my way. So, following in the footsteps of thousands of other seemingly aimless twenty-somethings, I decided to go back to school.

Being the impressionable youth I was, I thought back to all the lawyers I had seen on TV and decided I could be one too. Maybe that would be my "way." They seemed to have it together on the fancy lawyer shows. Of course, I could not afford it. I was only marginally less poor than in college, but I could at least take the LSAT and see what happened. What would be the harm except maybe setting myself up for another set of crushed hopes?

To my surprise, however, my brain had been conditioned to be over-analytical; reading the room in fear of being attacked also meant I could read practically any situation for a solution, both at my job and apparently on a written test other people spent years fretting over. With a careless effort, I managed to score off the charts out of dumb luck. Scholarship offers rolled in unexpectedly thanks to an ability to weave the compelling narrative of my personal tragedies into an essay that guilted wealthy schools into giving me money. My past could serve a purpose, after all. I wrote my own ticket and ended up at Columbia Law School in New York City.

Apparently, I had a type when it came to institutions of higher learning. Columbia was prestigious. People like me did not usually get into places like this. This was a place for other, better people, people of privilege. The walls virtually oozed with self-satisfaction, superiority, and authority. I had never felt any of those things, but lingering memories of my collegiate compatriots' indifference and full-throated confidence at DePauw and USC remained. Columbia beckoned with opportunity. Was this really a chance to start over a third time? Maybe now, with a few lessons under my belt, things would be different. I would start fresh, make new friends, and build some semblance of self. Columbia, it was.

I told the parents. They insisted on taking me out to dinner with the family to a Mexican restaurant nicknamed Peter's, after the owner, who knew everyone's order by heart. The 1950s had not ended in America; they had retired to Pasadena. The meal was nothing remarkable, of course. We'd gone there before and would go again. But on the car ride back, sandwiched between Robbie and his mother, with his sister in the front seat with his father, my life changed once and for all, a bookend to the ski trip a year prior.

"So, what are you doing with all your stuff when you move to New York?" Kathy asked.

"Oh, I don't know. My lease is up in May, so I'll go month to month and then put the rest in storage."

"Don't be silly," she said with that matter-of-fact tone she used when things were clear to her but quite the opposite to the rest of us. "Just move it into the guest house." The home they had purchased down the street from me a few years ago came with a small brick cottage on the property, which had lain empty for some time.

"I couldn't," I replied. I had spent my life trying not to burden people, and this fear had turned into a compulsion manifested into some serious emotional issues. The thought of storing my possessions in an empty guest house that wasn't mine absolutely terrified me for its sense of commitment and its acceptance of generosity.

"I absolutely couldn't," I said emphatically. "I'll figure it out. It's easy, there's no reason to put all that stuff there."

Kathy grew darkly serious. She was always light and happy, surefooted and kind, but in rare moments, the serious woman who had seen some serious shit in life came through. "Let me tell you something," she said. "When your mother tells you to do something, you do it. You are moving into the guest house. You will not waste money on rent when your lease expires. You will live with us when you are home during law school. And when you finish, you will live in the guest house until you buy your own home. No child of mine is going to throw away money on rent. You will live with us until you're ready for a house of your own."

I was speechless.

"Rob!" she shouted to her husband in the front seat. "Tell him there are no other options!"

In retrospect, she must have discussed this with her beloved husband, but he was the quiet one, and it did not occur to me she was doing anything other than leading the way. "You do what the boss tells you to do," the father said.

"So!" she said, cheering up and returning to her light-hearted tone, having gotten her way. "That's settled then?"

I had no choice but to nod. So that's what I did.

In the span of three minutes, it would turn out, the previous five years collapsed into a stellar explosion the extent of which I would only realize later. For days afterwards, I assumed simply it was an offhand comment and avoided further discussion. At most, I believed, it was a generosity that just meant my clothes would be in cardboard boxes in the back of the garage with the spare bed available when I came to Los Angeles. But in the months that followed, Kathy made it very clear it was anything but that.

She insisted on my move-in dates. She insisted I come "home" from New York every chance I got. She insisted that family holidays would include me. Photoshoots that had, in the past, taken place with just "the family" now took place with me. I had finally been fully welcomed into this weird grouping of oddly blessed and imperfectly perfect people. That night after Peter's, though, I would not truly see it until years later: those people had become my parents. Robbie had become my brother, and Kelley and Kristen had become my sisters. No transition would be perfect; it would take time before my newfound siblings absorbed the depth and seriousness of my mother's commitment. But they, too, would come to be closer than any blood had ever allowed in my life.

The thing I had been striving for my entire existence, to be wanted, to belong, to be loved, had suddenly happened while I had been drifting. You cannot undo twenty-four years of trauma, heartbreak, and madness in a single car ride, but it would all take a giant leap there, that moment. No amount of hugs or comforting nights with a glass of Nebbiolo would give me the skills I needed to move forward in life in any manner approaching classification as "emotionally healthy," but now, at least I truly had *something*. I had a family.

In a few short weeks, I'd enter a new school, my third institution of higher education, and try my luck again at a fresh start, the important difference being now that I had a family to back me up and I was not alone in the world.

I would not fully understand what a safety net was or even how to easily accept the help it offers. "The originals" had shown me what the anti-family was like, and it almost killed me. But now I had a mom and a dad and a brother and sisters who cared about me and who I had developed deep connections to…a real family. As I learned, sometimes small connection is all that separates a life of near madness from a one where you can walk into the tempest with new resolve, strengthened by fear but with your head held high.

CHAPTER 12

LEGALLY BLONDE

I prepped for Columbia Law School as any sane person would, you know—like Elle Woods in *Legally Blonde*. When I had worked at MGM, I absconded with a *Legally Blonde* DVD gift set with the original and sequel and a heart-shaped notepad and pink fluffy pen. I had decided Elle Woods was my spirit animal. I had studied for the LSAT with a casual indifference on Saturdays in the afternoon. Once enrolled, I extended my casual approach to my classwork. I figured everything I needed to know would become clear over time—there was nothing to worry about. "What, like it's hard?" I didn't have any legal ambition, anyway. Law school was only an impulsive and casual option to end the weird nothingness of my world and to kill some time.

As I sat in the second row on the first day of "Legal Methods" at Columbia Law School, a three-week introduction for new students, I did so with my *Legally Blonde* pen and notepad. If the esteemed Professor Ginsburg, daughter of the Supreme Court Justice, noticed my frivolity, she didn't let on. But the entire class and rest of the school did, and I wanted them to.

Years of trying to reinvent myself over and over throughout my undergraduate career had taught me what I thought were a few key lessons about life. To start, first impressions were everything. People usually don't take time to get to know you, even in the most generous of circumstances. I needed to make carefully planned, bold moves early to send the right message. Second, being fun was way more important than being smart. I had to be the smart kid to get scholarships, and that money was the way out of my hell. But at the end of the day, life showed me the question really was, who did you want to get high or drink or play poker with? Better to be the buddy, not the brain. Third, and most importantly, *do not* pitch yourself—let others do it for you. Build a reputation.

If this all sounds a little calculated, it was—it had to be. Law school might have been casual, but the life around it was not. I may have had a family, but I still didn't have an authentic vision of myself, so I was going to have to create one. I needed to buy some time to figure out who I was, and I had chosen to start with law school to do that. I had no intention of being a lawyer. I was there to make friends and enjoy a reprieve from my troubles for once. After drifting for years, this was a moment of respite. I was going to make it work with a new personality that made people smile. A personality that would give me value.

I woke up every day resolved to win over my classmates and professors. I stopped by office hours with invented questions and a cheerful Californian attitude. I attended every reception and club meeting with a big smile and a good story. I shared every funny anecdote I could think of. I had worked in Hollywood and had some singular experiences; I knew the people in movies everyone wanted to talk about. I created a public persona that was charming, gracious, and chatty. Since I had no interest in being a lawyer, I was not a professional threat to the other students. It should have been a winning formula…but it didn't seem to "take." As I walked the frosted-glass walls of Jerome Greene Hall, I was still missing something.

Just a few weeks into the semester, what I was missing would become very clear. One night, as I navigated the room at a reception, drinking the free red wine, I did what I thought one did in these social situations: engage in shallow banter.

"What's your name?" I'd repeat endlessly as I approached a continuing array of new fellow female students in knee-length, off-the-rack skirts.

"Laura." "Kathryn." "Leah." "Aviva."

The men had their own ill-fitting uniform of khakis and dated bland button downs.

"Gabe."

"Kevin."

"Max."

"Are you excited to be here? I mean, how crazy. I wonder what class is going to be like. What do you think the first assignment is?" I searched for something we could bond over.

"Assignment?" Leah stared at me, confused.

"Yeah, like worksheets, papers, I don't know. Like how they grade you?" I asked.

Leah scoffed and rolled her eyes. Her expression was a combination of indifference and smug superiority; it was enough to melt me on the spot. I may have been the same age as most of my classmates, but it seemed they had years of experience on me. In a single moment, I felt all those same feelings of not belonging from childhood, high school, and college all over again. Despite all my machinations, I had inadvertently revealed exactly what I was making this whole effort to hide. I was an outsider who didn't belong, and she was going to make sure I was fully briefed on that situation.

"There are no *worksheets* in law school," she sneered as she exactingly explained this new world to me. "There are cases, and there are exams. Your entire grade is based on an exam. And the cases are in the syllabus, which has been posted on the G drive for weeks."

Posted? G Drive? I didn't even know there was something called a G drive, and I didn't get to ask before Leah clicked her heels and marched off in search of someone more her intellectual peer. It was all news to me...everything. But she seemed totally confident about it all—didn't even need to give it a second thought, just like breathing. Everyone was like that, in fact.

Over the course of the night, I listened in on conversations, but in that awkward way where you approach to introduce yourself but are kept on the outside perimeter of the circle. I might as well have been a ghost. For all the talking they did, none of it was to me, nor did I try to contribute. Listening in, however, told me I was in for a rude awakening.

Law school was not what I thought it was going to be. I'm not even sure why I thought it would be so, having invented some vision in my head. But these people were ambitious and didn't pay attention to those who were not. Everyone seemed "in" on the law school jargon, like "PIN Cite" or "certiorari." Most had worked at law firms and were confident about their journey to professor, clerk, or partner. They knew who the teachers were down to the details of one case or another. These students had plans and goals, and they were on a mission. They were almost militaristic in their devotion to the Columbia Law School brand, a brigade of intensely focused cadets, no matter what their background or perspective. These kids (and we were all really still kids) enjoyed having late night discussions about legal principles like habeas corpus or the five elements of a tort, which to this day I have never learned. They obsessed over the guest lecturer on constitutional law in Estonia, just to give you an idea of what I'm talking about. Unlike everyone I had ever met and patterned my life after, they wanted to be smart, not fun. They wanted to philosophize, not play. They wanted rigor, not respite. Damn.

In a shocking twist for a guy who had been hellbent on being popular and fun, I had landed in a school where popularity was not part of the program and, unlike myself, the vast majority of my classmates had "discovered" themselves already. They were not interested in the guy with the fluffy pink pen from *Legally Blonde*, if they even cared enough to get the joke at all.

It would be just my luck all my plans seemed to run smack into a wall. These people seemed drab, dreary, and overly prepared, blinded by fear of not getting a job at a top law firm or an Appeals Court clerkship. They wanted to be the selves they had already found, not waiting around for someone else to find his. It seemed we had nothing in common. Even my cheery Californian affectation was a roadblock to their requisite seriousness. The reputation I had sought and promoted was not going to be well received.

To top it all off, they especially despised my carefree mentality. Students were scared of Columbia Law School and its immense footprint on 116th Street and Amsterdam Avenue. Beautiful marble and brick walks were fine, but they were terrified about future grades that served as a Sorting Hat of No Return. I had not even known how grades were determined, so I did not understand why someone might be afraid. It turned out the exam questions and *answers* were given out beforehand. It also seemed that everyone got As and Bs no matter what, along with the same salary at the same version of an old, white, male law firm or an old, white, male clerkship. It was baffling to me what everyone was worried about and why no one wanted to focus on making friends and having some fun. I truly was Elle Woods in a bunny costume, and I was at the wrong party.

Fuck. The three weeks of introductory Legal Methods went by very slowly. But I had one last shot, a tactic I had used in college with success: get everyone drunk. This would be my big play, a chance to overrun their Maginot Line of seriousness.

I convinced my roommate Greg to throw a party with me on the last day of Legal Methods. We spent the week dismantling our dining room and building a complete bar, taps included. Greg was down for anything that didn't require reading, and my shop classes in high school finally came in handy, putting it all together. I even added a bar wing that you flip up to get behind the bar with the idea everyone could sign it as an act of camaraderie.

Thankfully, even uptight law students will celebrate at the end of their first class, and it seemed free alcohol never loses its appeal, even if its source was from the "weird Californian kid." We didn't need décor or Christmas lights to make the place look special. We just removed half the lightbulbs to create the right dim ambiance, opened the bar, and provided endless red Solo cups. Being social chair had taught me people will keep coming, and stay, as long as the cups keep coming too.

As the night rolled on, my classmates rolled with it. Even "know how it works" Leah was there. Jake, Noel, Jeff, David, Barbara, Deanna, LaRue, and Julian. Beca, Kathryn and Katherine, Tina, Hadi, Brandon, Ben. I would get to know them all in the years that followed in different ways, but tonight they were all cogs in a giant image rehab machine. This was to be the night people gave me a shot at being part of the group.

There were so many people in our tiny apartment that they began to spill out into the stairwell. Someone saw the door to the roof was not alarmed, so the party moved up and outside. More than a hundred people, a third of my class, were now milling about on a hot summer night, celebrating that "we made it," as if the end of three-week pass-fail course where everyone passes was an achievement.

As people drank, they *really* drank, and they let it all out. They revealed all the things they'd been hiding for the last three weeks. It turns out they did have emotions and fears after all. They were just not sharing them because I was different. I didn't know whether to be angry or relieved that there was an entire universe I had been cut off from and I was just finding out about it. Trying to be funny and popular had made me the opposite. I was not what they had expected in law school, and they apparently didn't know what to do with me. As I made the rounds, the feedback was revealing.

"You're from Hollywood, dude," Jake explained. "Who the fuck here knows anything about Hollywood? You're speaking a completely different language. Like, you bought Snoop Dogg weed." He shrugged. "And I don't even know what to do with that information."

"You're gay, but it's weird because you don't talk about it," Matt explained. I would bed him that night and for the next several weeks, but for now, he just told me that apparently the "other gays" felt I didn't belong because I didn't broadcast my sexuality. "They think you think you're better than them or that you're hiding something."

The secrets and insights flowed like cheap wine from a box. I discovered that over the last three weeks, I had been operating in isolation and had apparently opted out or been excluded from every group of friends in law school without knowing it. I was just trying to be what I thought was a fun, typical student. To everyone else, I was different. Columbia Law School was the land of misfit toys for people who wanted to become cogs in a system, and I was the blond boy from California who made no sense. I pumped classmate after classmate for information, only to find out they each had new reasons for keeping me on the outside.

There were definitely cliques, and not just the judgmental gay men. There were the bros, guys who, in another context, would be on a flag football team pounding beers. They had ended up in law school because their WASP fathers said that it was what "their" sort of people did to end up with the picket fence and two kids. Clearly, not me.

The Erudite: the future judges of America, planning to join Law Review and become journal editors. They seemingly prized knowledge and loved philosophic arguments about legal minutia. Definitely not me. They also thought I was stupid, so there was that. Jokes about the movie *First Daughter* and dancing with Mandy Moore made me superficial.

The list goes on: the do-gooders, the feminists, the international students, even cliques based on the smallest of things, like tort reform. I suppose these groups also existed in college, but in a class of three hundred, they were much more apparent. There were also regular people, like how I saw myself, with whom I might have made friends if not for something unidentifiable in the ether. They would be the ones I'd have to pursue.

Life came into focus on that warm Manhattan night as I worked the room. People began talking to me instead of around me, even if the things they said were just simply awful at times. What people reveal when they are wasted can be truly astonishing. I mean, who would actually tell the "weird one" what everyone really thought of him? My fellow law students, that's who. Apparently, law school causes you to lose all tact when it comes to someone else's feelings. On the verge of crying, I drank instead. A lot.

I drank while I listened to a dowdy English girl talk about having been fucked and tossed away by my roommate after she thought she was in love with him. I drank as I listened to Matt tell me the gay guys were telling him to stay away from me, while he stuck his hand down my back pocket. I drank as Leah told me about the rich older guy her parents wanted her to marry back in Los Angeles, but she had hopes of finding a "nice Jewish man" in New York.

I drank all through my one-night education in how law school really worked. In retrospect, I should have read a blog; it would have been easier on my emotions.

I was told I was doing everything backwards. I didn't treat class as an exercise in transcription, I didn't have a laptop, and I didn't "case outline." These were all normal parts of law school, as was joining a clinic or a journal or any number of things future lawyers did, and everyone knew the checklist except me. Why would I do any of this if I didn't want to be a lawyer? Perhaps that was actual the death knell to my law school ambitions, I finally realized.

"Who goes to law school if they don't want to become a lawyer?" Dave, one of the Bros, asked me. "That's just fucked up." What I thought had made me non-threatening also made me stand out in a bad way. "Like, you took someone else's spot that really could have done something with it." He stared blankly at me, his vision obviously beginning to blur.

I excused myself to "check on" someone who didn't exist and went back down to my apartment. I stood in my bedroom, music blaring outside, audible through the thin bedroom door. Sitting on my little bed and cheap sheets, I stared at the off-white walls. There wasn't a single poster or photo on them, and there never would be. Decorating was an emotional investment I did not want to make. The emptiness was indicative of my life at the moment, a lot of wall but all empty. As I pondered what might become of me in this crazy place, I also realized that as much as that night hurt, it made things at law school much clearer. These people really were all the same as everyone else, driven by different end goals, to be sure, but with many of the same insecurities, desires, and motivations as USC fraternity brothers or DePauw undergraduates.

Mason wanted the life his dad had, a good career, and most importantly, a picture-perfect family. Matt was a puppy searching for an American husband and with it, an identity. Luke was a lost boy looking for answers, displaced from the close-knit family he had always known. Drab Lauren was just looking for someone to love her for more than the cheap Zara clothes she easily tossed on a different bedroom floor every night.

Everybody wanted something, everybody had some insecurity, and everybody was a little like me, and I was noting every single detail. Of course, they all did indeed have a spartan-like, hardcore plan for Columbia, and that *was* weird. But the alcohol revealed they were just all play-acting too. These people were the cream of the crop. They came from the best schools and the best families and had all the preparation and care in the world to be ready for this moment. Yet here they were, one hundred messes on a rooftop pretending to be something they were not and keeping me on the outside. I can now understand how they, too, were terrified of not achieving their own dreams.

I may not have known what law school was like going in, but that could be fixed. Perhaps it was just vodka cranberry-fueled confidence, but suddenly every verbal jab didn't hurt as it did in the past. I did not feel defeated or want to run away. I felt motivated as I went back to the party. These people were all going by the rules of some unwritten book. If I could use that book to my advantage, in addition to the things I had learned from all those years spent observing instead of living, I could *make* something of this place.

I did make something of my time there. My party was just the start. Our "bar" became a student watering hole with regular gatherings. Free alcohol was an enticement, and information became payment. But I had a limited budget and needed more resources, which, it turns out, law school had a ready answer for.

I started my own student organization, the California Society, and used it to turn one bar night into a something that would play a large part in my law school world. It was nominally to promote the interests of and topics related to Californian students, but having my own little entity allowed me to access student programming funds and raise my own money for CalSoc, as it was nicknamed.

The International Law Society may have been content to raise ten thousand dollars to throw a few luncheons with pizza and a yearly conference, but I wanted to fry bigger fish. Coming from the land of endorsements, I slapped a name on any program I could create. They were real programs, of course: The XYZ Law Firm Mentoring Program, the ABC Law Firm Career Day. But they were vehicles to raise hundreds of thousands of dollars, which I had almost complete control over. And where there is money, there is opportunity, even in a tiny law school world.

My organization's money allowed me to become the social, career, and activities chair who fulfilled every student's need. If they wanted something, I'd be the best (and eventually only) shop in town. I held the best lunch-and-learns. I threw the best parties. I took everyone's hopes and desires for their top ten law firm jobs and clerkships and created the most important career days, providing exclusive access to the people they wanted most. I tied both firms and students into CalSoc and used those ties to build a world that matched the one I wanted. If Columbia Law School was a place I did not fit in, I could make it into one where I did.

Sure, some people truly wanted the programming I created, but eventually, it simply became a movement one could not avoid. Even people who resented CalSoc joined because they had to, as we amassed resources, access, and success. I was able to use those resources to remake everything I could outside the classroom. As one not-so-kind blog commenter wrote, I "took Columbia from being a place where it mattered what you knew to a place where it mattered who you knew and how cool you were." Deep philosophical legal discussions of the elements of a tort be damned.

At that first party, a new version of me had been born. In that moment, as campus security shut us down and we retreated to the Lion's Head Tavern, I embraced my plan and all that it entailed. As I knocked back "Irish Car Bomb" shots at the bar with my roommate and inebriated classmates, I realized there was a chance I could do all of this. I may have been on the outside, but a door had opened, and I was going to jump through it as I embraced a gargantuan effort to remake my world around me.

A realization took hold of me: if I could not be someone else's idea of what normal was, maybe I could make "normal" look like me. That's not why I had come to law school, and it's not why I ran away as a child or why I parroted professors at DePauw or even why my new-found parents had supported me. The lessons I learned from my time in the mountains, the heartbreak around Andrew, and the loss of all I knew seemed to fade away without residue or regret. All those years to realize I could be something *other* than what I saw in everyone else.

Shockingly, I now realize, that journey fell to the wayside at the first taste of something I had sought since I sat eating cheap cookies in my childhood. Cravings, when finally satiated, however little, can reignite and burn for a thousand years. My original plans quickly faded as I became obsessed with "meaning" something and exerting even the tiniest bit of control over my life. As my obsession grew, it consumed me and would eventually nearly destroy me. It turned out chasing normal—whether someone else's version or my own—was a fool's errand, and I'd have to learn that lesson all over again.

CHAPTER 13

A BLONDE GIRL AND
A GINGER BOY

Law school and my quest to remake it was not the only journey I'd go on in New York City. I'd also discover the most intimate friendship I would ever have. Kate Harris was normal's idea of normal. She grew up in Laguna Beach, California, she was a student with me at USC, and she was a sister at Kappa Delta Delta directly across the street from my fraternity. KDD was at the top of the of sorority hierarchy, and Kate was one of its princesses. She embraced the two-tone life Kappa sisters exemplified: red-bottom shoes and green piles of cash. Her life checked off every box on the list: loving parents, an idyllic childhood, high-powered internships, the standard fraternity boyfriend, good job as an event-planner, skilled networker who made sure we had dinner once a quarter to "keep in touch." She was destined for whatever was Southern California's version of "high society," and she owned it: blonde hair, beauty, high heels, and all. The Stepford wives were copying her, not the other way around.

Then there was her exodus. The woman I knew in college, whose entire life had been mapped out for her, dropped it all and moved to New York to escape her self-imposed prison at the same time I went to Columbia Law School. She left behind everything she knew and started over from scratch. She networked her way into a much-sought-after job in fashion and then worked nose to the grindstone up the ladder. Her Stepford perfection allowed her to move in and out of friendships and into the most popular clubs. She used her beauty and her brains to land any guy she casted for and fillet them and have them in the skillet before they even knew what was happening.

Our quarterly check-ins from Los Angeles became weekly gossip sessions in New York. I got updates on her adventures when we met for coffee at the Pain Quotidien on West 72nd Street. Although we had not been close at USC, moving to New York at the same time inadvertently brought us together. The break from her past happened at the same time as mine, and her journey to self-discovery, even if shorter and less haphazard, gave us something to bond over.

Every Sunday, Kate would regale me with the stories from her weekend. What she was building made my tiny little enterprise at law school pale in comparison. I was working in a world of a few hundred students; Kate was rising in Manhattan's most exclusive social scene. She had a birthday party at a club that served cocktails in teacups and saucers and hosted dinners in a basement restaurant on the Lower East Side before anyone else knew it was trendy. She frequented

Employees Only and every other bar as if she were one of the owners. She had a standing reservation at La Esquina and a circle of girls who had found their church at Soul Cycle on Sundays. Kate was pretty, slender, and smart, with stunning blonde hair. She could own a room from the moment she walked in. She was the only girl I knew who said, "Don't hate the player, hate the game," and who saw it from both sides. She knew how to work the rules to her advantage every time.

She had come from privilege, but having fled it in Los Angeles, she made a new high-society bubble for herself in New York. If that's not landing on your red-soled shoes, I don't know what is. It was pluck and a hard-working attitude, but it was also the cultural capital one acquires as a normal girl from Laguna Beach. Initially, I was an entranced spectator, but our shared emotional journey brought us closer. I loved our Sundays together. I loved them for the stories. I loved them for the entrée. I loved them for the universe it opened to me, as her friend, to places I'd never known about and would otherwise never go. She might go to La Esquina every week, but going even once made me a topic of conversation in law school. Most of all, I loved our time for the close friendship between us and hearing how she felt about her life and her self-discovery. Law students closed me out, but Kate exposed me to an even bigger world, with a route that resembled my own but on a different, five-star level.

We shared some chapters in the book of life. This woman, who knew she was gorgeous, was still genuinely insecure about her nose. She seemed to play games with boys not because she wanted to be a player—she wasn't bouncing from bed to bed—but out of a sense of self-preservation. She hit up all the best social spots and Soul Cycle classes because she enjoyed them but also because she knew making a reputation, gaining access, and building a life required hard work. Going out every weekend, finding every hot spot, and getting to know every doorman was *work* that ensured results, just like any office job. Kate was owning New York, and from the outside, she was just like every hard-working successful woman. On the inside, she struggled just like I did. Those Sundays, talking with her, I learned I was not alone.

For the first time since Andrew, someone was truly, deeply opening up to me, even as we had fun. It was an odd experience, learning how to build a true friendship after twenty-four years, when most people had learned this sharing Play-Doh in pre-school or at the very least over sneaking beers in high school. Here I was, in law school, pretending my way through life along with someone else and sharing the quiet secret that lay beneath: perhaps there was more than meets the eye to her and me, and we were the only two who knew that about each other.

Kate was patient and kind and listened. But even as I opened up, I was careful to limit my exposure. Andrew remained a stark reminder how much it could hurt when you give yourself away; I was not prepared to do that again. Even as Kate shared some of her most intimate moments, I held back. So, every Sunday, she ordered coffee and told me about the latest guy chasing her down or the girl she had befriended at the new nightclub on Lafayette. I ordered hot chocolate, and at Pain Quo, that meant warm milk and a side of liquid chocolate, which Kate would eat with a spoon while

I told her about CalSoc as if it were of the same stature as her achievements.

One Sunday was different. I wanted to talk. I was about to cross a big bridge for the first time, and I had no idea what burden our new friendship might bear. I had decided to open up about a blossoming romance, my first real romance, something that was deeply personal and exciting in a totally new way. Civil procedure and the social politics of my little corner of Morningside Heights could be interesting, but it was not personal. And as deeply satisfying as remaking my law school was, it did not quicken my heart. But a guy had come along who had, and I wanted to share this with Kate. I had never shared such intimate feelings with a friend; it was surreal to think I even could.

I had never been in or out of the closet, really. When figuring out where your next meal was coming from was a daily problem, who you wanted to kiss was secondary. Years before, James had awakened a desire in me, which then Andrew blew into a roaring fire. Even as I finished college still bedding girl after girl, I was doing the same to guys in Hollywood, all without having a single conversation with anyone about gender, sexuality, or romance. No one seemed to ask, and no one I slept with really mattered.

My experiences tended toward the one-and-done, late at night when vodka-induced confidence gives shy people the extra oomph needed to overcome years of self-loathing in order to approach someone more attractive than themselves.

My self-loathing came from being poor and depressed, not being closeted. Kate never asked who I was having sex with, and I never said. But it wasn't the sex that mattered. It was the vulnerability, something I had started to learn from Kate. I decided to share with her that there was someone special I was also learning new things from.

Kate had been unknowingly present when I had met the boy, named Brian. Several weeks before, she had invited me to a USC football viewing party on Park Avenue South. USC might have been thousands of miles away, but alumni gathered rambunctiously every week during football season to take over bars with fans, chants, and cheers. For those from USC, it was a little bit of home away from home. For those who had been perpetually on the outside like me, it created a longing for what might have been. But that night, I sat there with Kate, her friends, and her mother visiting from out of town, and I felt like I was part of it all. I felt like I belonged to this little brigade, for whom the game's every down was a victory and every punt a crushing defeat. It was thrilling, and I was a fully engaged participant, egged on by Kate and comforted by her cheering right there with me.

My whole world changed in an instant. It happened when I saw Brian out of the corner of my eye. I caught a glimpse of a ginger-haired, pale white guy egging on his own table of friends but curiously, as an antagonist, a bold move in a bar filled with drunk Trojan football fans. I saw he was wearing a red shirt, like everyone else, but his had a Razorback on it, the opposing team mascot. As the evening wore on and USC began to trounce Arkansas, he lost interest in the game and began gazing round the room, when his eyes fell on me.

The thing to me about being a gay man is that it's pretty easy to spot another one, even in a crowded room, if you know how to see what is really going on. It's not about gait or tenor or tone or how perfect the hair. All of those stereotypes have some elements of truth, but for a gay man, the easiest way to spot one of your own was what I always thought of as "the gaze." It worked by finding someone, looking them directly in the eyes, and holding it just about four seconds, then giving off a smile. In my experience, a straight guy will turn away; a gay guy will smile back, and you've got about a 50 percent chance of ending up in bed later that night. For better or worse, that's how it used to work, though times have changed.

About halfway through the second quarter, the Ginger Boy caught my eye and smiled, and electricity shot up my spine. I had certainly slept with men since Andrew, and I had been sleeping with British Matt in law school since my Legal Methods party. This wasn't like that. I felt excitement, joy, and nervousness, all bound up at once. I would come to call this "the spark." I now know there are only few times in a life when it strikes, but at that moment, all I knew was this guy across the room was causing it, and I had to meet him.

The game droned on, the fans cheered, and I feigned interest in the conversations with Kate, her mom, and her friends, while my attention was squarely focused elsewhere. It was comical how many times I turned around to see my new crush and check out his smile. Even he seemed to be in on the joke, and we started mouthing things to each other, although all I caught for sure was that his name was Brian.

At halftime, I found myself in the men's bathroom line, and Brian was two people behind me. I was not going to let this chance to talk to him pass me by, no matter how nervous. As I smiled back at him and moved back to his place in the line, my heart was pounding. I could feel my face turning red and a burning sensation that pulsed inside my forehead as I struggled to say hi.

"I mean, who comes to a USC game to root for Arkansas?" I opened. Smart move, Craig. *Smart.* I berated myself for opening with an insult and in the split second before he responded debated a half dozen ways to explain I had been joking, or that I was socially awkward, or that I found rooting for any team good sportsmanship. It's remarkable the number of things you can come up with in your head in the space of a nanosecond. But Brian smiled and laughed, a laugh filled with the warm joy of one too many beers.

"I don't really care about Arkansas," he said. "I just hate USC. So, I bought this shirt just to root against them tonight."

"That's extreme," I shot back, leaning a bit closer to him. Our shoulders touched slightly, and a second shiver went up my spine. "Who goes to a USC game just to root against USC?"

Brian explained his friends were avid fans, and they were all from Hawaii but had ended up in New York together. He was attending grad school at NYU, Columbia's rival.

"We're bound to be enemies," I smirked.

We raced against time as the line in front of us for the bathroom got shorter and shorter until I finally had the courage to ask for his number just before I went in. I plugged his information into my cheap phone, while he did the same into a sleek new Razr, the kind that was all the rage back then. This guy had money, I remember thinking, and he was cute, and he seemed into me.

As I wound my way back to the table, a text popped up… and another, as I replied, and another. We kept staring across the room, waiting for the other to smile in reaction to the text banter, an inside joke across a crowded room just between us. A typical person would have run back to his table and filled everyone in, but I was skittish about anything personal, and my friendship with Kate was still new. So, for the moment, it was my little secret, and it was fun, thrilling, and sexual all at once. Back then, texting did not consist of chest or dick pics, nor did I have had any to send. Brian and I had experienced an old fashioned run-in and exchanged numbers and then engaged in actual conversation.

"Would you like to go on a constitutional?" he wrote.

"A what?" I wrote back, perplexed.

"It's a good old-fashioned walk. After the game."

"In," I replied.

I did not know what type of person Brian was, but so far, he had been cute, funny, and charming, and now he was using nineteenth-century vocabulary to invite me on a quasi-date. I was all in. I had been sleeping with Matt for a few weeks, but we had not gone on a single date. I had been hooking up with guys for years but not actually gone on a real date. All of a sudden, I was going to go on a tipsy walk around the streets of lower Manhattan, and I could not have been happier. As the game ended, Kate and her friends invited me to join them at the newest club. I begged off, which was unusual, and Kate saw it in my face. She asked me if everything was okay, and she could see something was different. But she let it go, and I waited for them to leave before turning around and accidentally bumping straight into Brian.

"Whoa, cowboy!" he said, his drunk voice pitching a little higher and giggling in a way I'd come to know and love.

"Ready?" he asked, smiling from ear to ear. He grabbed my hand without thinking, and off we set on our constitutional.

It was the first time anyone had ever grabbed or even held my hand affectionately in public. I was stunned. As Brian and I walked along the streets, he led confidently, talking about his life and asking me about mine. I was only half listening as I felt his palm in mine. He swung our hands back and forth and squeezed mine a little tighter every now and then as if to remind me this was a conscious effort, not a casual one.

Pieces of my life flashed in my mind, sketches in contrast to Brian's picture-perfect anecdotes. I had no point of reference for a friendly hug from a mom or friends gossiping with each other late into the night. And here, next in the long line of things Craig knew nothing about, never expected, and had no baseline response for, was a twenty-two-year-old guy from Hawaii holding my hand and smiling as he chatted about his French major at NYU. I started to fall in love that very moment, and that spark became a catalyst for weeks of pure joy.

We went home together that night and stayed up talking and fooling around, although not having sex, which was unusual for me. I usually dove in quickly, never allowing emotions to develop. It was easier if it was only about sex from the start, but this time was clearly different. He invited me to stay and have lunch with him the next day and dinner two nights later. He planned dates and outings, and I took the train to see him almost every other day for weeks. We'd stay up late watching *Battlestar Galactica* and talking about nonsense. We rushed forward with all the abandon that comes with youth, the kind that doesn't ask whether you're spending too much time together or playing "the game" correctly. Andrew Russ may have been my first love, but I didn't know it when it was happening. With Brian, I felt it in real time. I sensed it to my core, and he did too.

For the first time in my life, I was feeling a reciprocal romance, and like CalSoc, my new parents, or my friendship with Kate, it was like I was suddenly discovering all these wonderful parts of life that had been closed off by some magical wall. If this is what growing up had been like for other people, how could they ever be lonely or sad or disappointed? If this is what others had because they were not fighting for a dollar for food or hiding out in the library before school started, then what in high heaven were they doing in life? Admittedly, I would later realize life and emotions are more complex, but at the moment, I was with a man I knew was falling in love with me—"smitten," he would call it—and I with him. Even our rare arguments were easily smoothed over as young lovers do, ignoring red flags as they get to know each other.

One night early in our time together, we were walking home from dinner at French Roast, a café around the corner from his well-appointed apartment in the West Village. He ran ahead, crossed one foot over the other, and leapt into the air, clicking his heels. He laughed uproariously. I asked what that was for.

"You!" He giggled. "You make me feel like doing that all the time!"

To this day, that memory still rips my heart apart. I had been so lonely, so bereft, so adrift without an anchor. I had been abandoned by the parents God had assigned to me, isolated from friends. I resorted to being the most useful person in the room just to make sure I had value, yet here was a man actually jumping for joy because of me.

As I sat there a week later, telling Kate this story, it felt as if no words could express what I was feeling. Every phrase felt trite, and even though I was ardently, passionately plumbing the depths of my heart, it felt as if no one would understand. She smiled and seemed to share in my joy but only to a certain extent. At that point in her life, Kate had not yet felt her own "spark" for someone yet. Nonetheless, my worries about sharing my new relationship with her abated as she accepted my vulnerability with kindness and support.

Decades before, I had run away from everything and everyone I knew with a plate of cookies in my hand, only have to slink back to reality. I had done the same thing at USC, filled with terror that the small semblances of a stable reality I had were being torn away. Now I had parents, I had a friend who listened and shared, and for the first time, I had a boyfriend who loved me. I had made a life at Columbia, though artificially constructed and on precarious ground. I had something resembling an identity. I thought this would be a solid foundation for the first time.

This foundation was not built on mimicking others or how I thought I should be but on what I thought I wanted to be. And that was a start. But sometimes when life hands you these feelings, it tests them and takes them away, as had repeatedly happened to me. These were realer joys, deeper moments, better truths. But I had been through enough smaller versions to wonder if this would fall apart like before.

Here I was, finally making a go of it, but I had been close before. Would this time be different? And if so, why? I faced a question I never had before in all the difficulties and hardships I had endured: was it repeating because of me? Was I in a cycle of my own inadvertent creation, or had I finally made a leap forward absent the terrors that had plagued me for so long?

I didn't see the signs that night standing there with Brian, but I felt the lingering effects of my anxiety. Perhaps I was chasing something that wasn't meant for me anyway. I thought chasing other peoples' idea of normal that had been the problem, but it wasn't so simple. Trying to follow my own desires in New York had seemed like a solution, but I had no way of knowing if Brian, Kate, or even my fledgling new parents were going to last. If it were possible to be caught between love and terror, I was. I rushed up to Brian and kissed him, trying to hold back my tears. Those tears would sustain me over the next two years until all my questions were answered by a crisis that threatened to undo me and all my work for something stable, honest, and real.

CHAPTER 14

ON THE OUTSIDE LOOKING IN

S torms can appear suddenly on the horizon, even if you are watching for them. They are the product of a complex interaction of wind, air pressure, moisture, temperature, and even the earth's rotation. As I was living in New York, all the same sort of powerful forces of a storm were brewing right in front of me, even though I never really saw it coming.

CalSoc gained momentum and grew and so did my hubris around my standing and influence, which I felt had reached to every corner of the school. I was put in charge of Dean's Cup, a high-profile inter-law school event between Columbia and NYU. I operated from the back bench of the student senate, serving as a miniature Churchill, excoriating what I saw as lunacy coming from those who were focused only on getting prestigious clerkships. Still, nothing going on in law school mattered as much as my friendship with

Kate or the joy I experienced flying home to see my new parents in Los Angeles and the warm embrace of my first boyfriend. I should have paid more attention to the dark clouds forming above the law school at West 116th Street and Amsterdam Avenue.

In the meantime, while the storm was gathering in the distance, I learned some other hard lessons, even from the people and things that had brought me joy. In the midst of my still-chaotic world, Brian invited me to spend New Year's Eve with him at home in Hawaii. Thankfully, Columbia had awarded me a full scholarship so I could accept his invitation, having been able to save money from still working on the side. I remember thinking, "So this is what normal people are like. They fly to see their boyfriends and spend New Year's Eve with friends." I had never been to a party I hadn't hosted, and growing up, I certainly did not have friends I spent holidays with.

I was going to *experience* something *normal* firsthand. My entire life, I had been the penniless kid on the outside of the bakery, looking in through a thick plate of glass. I could see all the cakes and cookies and deliciousness that a life filled with love, money, meaning, and friends could bring, but I was never allowed inside. The most I could do was watch those people coming and going, seeing how they behaved, what they ordered, and the delight that came with every bite. I stood outside, never allowed in, mimicking their actions, holding a hand full of air, and pretending it was a piece of the most delicious cake with exquisite frosting made of the most exclusive butter from a tiny little town in France. Or so

I would have been, if the bakery had been real and Dickens had been writing the scene.

The mimicry was real, however, as was looking from the outside in. I was studying everything: Kevin's nonchalance, Kate's confidence, the phrases and behavior of fellow students. I had seen what I thought were the results of being normal, even if I had never really internalized it at all. I remember that in high school, for example, I was taken by a teacher to a sushi dinner with a group of students to celebrate our graduating at the top of the class. I watched intently as everyone deftly maneuvered their chopsticks to eat the little pieces of fish. Although sushi in a nearly landlocked state is never a good idea, I wanted to appear like everyone else but had no idea how to use those little sticks of wood. I spent a half a damn hour trying to get one piece to my mouth. Never has so little food tasted so good. Exhausted from the social anxiety and fearful of dropping a second piece, I didn't eat anything for the rest of the night. Now, with Brian in Hawaii, I would be like those kids were back then, living a normal moment, knowing what the right technique was for success.

From the moment I arrived in Hawaii, Brian did all the things that made me fall in love with him in the first place. He was excited and giggly just seeing me. (I really loved his high-pitched laugh.) He was thrilled for me to meet his family. He had made all sorts of plans to show me his beloved hometown of Kailua. I was on cloud nine as he presented me with a lei and cracked the inevitable jokes about how happy he was to get me "lei'ed" in Hawaii. As we drove through Oahu towards his home, dancing in the car, I was actually experiencing what other people had told me about. But this was the first time I really felt it myself. It was Brian and his love for me that made me feel as if I belonged, if only for a moment.

We went to his favorite shave ice shop and his favorite lunch spot. We even visited his elementary school, Punahou. He took me by his father's properties, and I discovered where Brian's two-bedroom apartment in the West Village came from: his father was an executive at one of the largest property holding companies in Hawaii. Then, toward the end of the day, he finally brought me home to meet his parents.

His mother, Ingrid, greeted us at the door. Her bright blue eyes, filled with joy, shone out from under her hair, bleached by decades in the sun. As she hugged me, I felt the warmth Brian must have felt his entire life. I heard the tenor in her voice as her children and their friends sprung through the house like deer bounding through the forest. We had dinner and sat around playing games, talking and laughing as neighbors and friends popped in and out. It was like Grand Central Station; someone was always coming or going, and yet Ingrid and Brian's dad were unflappable. They were Auntie and Uncle to everyone (these were terms of affection in Hawaii) and their home was a neighborhood gathering spot, way station, and information center all at once. I never once saw them get upset, although I'm sure they did once in a while. And as much as I had my new parents now, that was still a recent development. This was immersion in Brian's world, and it was magical.

As the week passed, we did every touristy thing imaginable, from visiting the Battleship Missouri to the Iolani Palace, going from war games to playing king and king. It was kitschy fun and was just about us. It seemed like a montage from some romcom movie, the most normal thing I could have imagined. Even being caught inside during a Hawaiian downpour felt so typical and so special at the same time.

One night, we lay there in his room, listing to the raindrops hit hard outside the paper-thin walls as we waited for dinner. He cuddled me as we lay on the floor, laughing intermittently, telling me about his life, his love, his world. I learned about his freewheeling and curious childhood, of the purple utility food named "poi" that everyone talked about, and how his parents had maintained a sense of warmth in their home. He was so self-assured. He wasn't overconfident or arrogant, but fulfilled. He had a three-part tattoo on his ankle in tribute to his two best friends growing up, symbolizing their friendship. This kind of parenting, this kind of friendship, this kind of world...I had seen it from a distance my whole life. I had only begun to experience a little bit of it with my parents and Kate. But laying there in his arms, I could pretend I was a part of this world, my own version of *The Little Mermaid*. Perhaps I could be forgiven for world-building in those moments, thinking how his parents would become my in-laws someday, his best friends, mine. There was a shout from the kitchen that dinner was ready, and the spell was broken. That was as close as I would come that trip to thinking that believing could become being.

Alas, as my visit proceeded, I started to feel things shifting under the surface of our relationship. As New Year's Eve approached, Brian became preoccupied with his friends and their plans. The shine was wearing off the illusion of this trip being just about us. He went from being carefree and spontaneous to rigidly planning out every detail for the whole group. No one could seem to agree, and his lighthearted laughs turned into grunts of frustration. I would later discover this was a normal part of friendships, healthy disagreements that reconciled through hugs and beers later.

His behavior was triggering to me at the time, but I kept my mouth shut, even when he snapped at me in the grocery store for picking out the wrong mixers. As I tried to move past his moods, however, I saw that I was figuring less and less into Brian's considerations and plans. His decisions were about what he and the friends wanted; he didn't ask me what I might like. My presence on the trip suddenly became secondary. It was as if once we had ticked off the museums and photo opportunities, I was expected to fall into the plans for his life without question or modification. I was blending into his normal, not creating one for both of us. It was a precursor to the conflicts that broke us up some months later. First loves don't always last forever. But in that moment, his forgetfulness was a price I was willing to pay, if only temporarily, thinking he would come around once the holiday arrived.

The holiday did arrive, and I was wrong—things did not change. As we bounced from house party to club and back again, I was dragged along for the ride as Brian ran us around on his perfect night. Beer pong now, this tiki bar next, then to another club, and back to the beer pong house. It was like riding in a car with someone who was changing the radio station every five minutes.

I pushed back once as we were leaving yet another club decked in streamers and cheap confetti, looking for the "right crowd" and the "right friends."

"Brian, it's okay, we can stay here," I implored. "It seems fun."

"There is no one here," he grunted, frustrated at the lack of crowd. "They said it would be a good spot." He tapped away on his silver phone, trying to find more friends.

"I'm sure it will be good. It's early. Let's just stay and dance."

"No, we can do better.... Oh! Sterling says he found something," he replied, referencing an incoming text from one of his friends we'd spent the night chasing after.

My feelings didn't really matter to him in that moment, no matter how much I knew he loved me. We spent the rest of the night running from party to party and eventually fell asleep at a house Sterling had rented.

The next morning, I was dehydrated and parched with a hangover, feeling the pain of a night spent in a vodka-fueled party marathon. I woke first and stared at Brian as he slept. There's nothing like the quiet snoring of a drunken body next to you to break a romantic trance. Brian woke and smiled at me.

"Did you have fun?" he asked, bleary-eyed. I smiled and assured him I had. But it wasn't true.

The trip had been fun at first. I had relished being special to him and seeing all the plans he made for me. I had embraced his family and felt their warm feelings in return. I felt like I had belonged. I was his boyfriend, and his world had become my world, and it was like we were building something together. His normal was mine too until it wasn't. Being a part of normal for a moment wasn't the same as belonging there forever or building a future together. I had experienced firsthand the life I had seen from a distance throughout the years and come away almost empty-handed. The only thing I took away was the painful realization, however small, that I did not belong to Brian's world, and that critical fact meant we would not be together for much longer. I suppose first loves are often destined to be brief but intense, but that did not make it any less painful. For me, glimpsing the world I had wanted for so long made the loss all the more gut-wrenching.

There's a scene in a collection of short stories by Ray Bradbury called *The Machineries of Joy*. In it a man creates a machine designed to bring happiness. One goes inside, and it shows pictures of the most beautiful people and places in the world, the reasoning being that you would be so overwhelmed by the beauty and joy you see, you would be filled with happiness. For his first outing, the inventor takes his machine to the woman he thinks needs it most, his wife, a mother with five or six children, trapped in an endless cycle of cooking, cleaning, toddler screams, and broken toys. Willing to hear the inventor out but skeptical, she steps into the machine. A few minutes go by, and then a few more. Then, after a while, tears can be heard from inside. The man, concerned, opens the door to see his wife sobbing.

"What could be wrong?" he asks her, aghast at her state. "Did I not show you all the most beautiful things in the world?"

She looks up at him, anger and sadness in her eyes.

"Yes," she says. "And although I knew my life was not great before, I did not think of the things I was missing. I had not seen them. Now that I have, my life is filled with sadness."

The experience of seeing firsthand what made other people so happy yet knowing it was not going to last and did not belong to her, and that it was better than the life she led and would lead, brought her the most profound sadness.

Now, knowing what I experienced in Hawaii, I desperately worried I, too, would be relegated to the same fate as I boarded the plane for home, my eyes filled with tears.

CHAPTER 15

ONE LAST MISTAKE

My escape to Hawaii was a lesson in how life can turn on you. A little more than two years after Hawaii, I was going to face an even bigger crisis, and I made a series of tragic mistakes once again. It seemed then that all my mistakes were coming home to roost at the same time. The storms of my world finally came in.

I sat on the stoop of my apartment building in New York with my standard-issue black law school backpack lying on the ground in front of me. It was dark outside, and the chilly winds clipped my face, signaling the turning of fall to winter. My relationship with Brian was very far in the rearview mirror, as were a few less consequential ones. After nine months, Brian and I had eventually accepted an end that was nothing like our first happy "constitutional." I suppose, like many youthful romances, after a fast and furious courtship, we realized if we had known each other as well at the start as we did at the end, we would never have gotten together. After Brian, I had moved on from one man to the next, until I arrived at the one sitting across from me this chilly fall night, Kyle.

At the moment, in my somewhat damaged emotional state, Kyle seemed no different from any of his predecessors, and so I shed no tears as he embraced his own sorrow at our breakup. I listened to him telling me how "unavailable and distant" I was, how he didn't know what to do to "reach me," so he didn't think we could keep seeing each other. It struck me at the moment, he didn't know why I was distant. I had not told him the basic, and most traumatizing, essentials of my life as they had been happening, including the fact that I was facing expulsion from law school. Distant, yes, and distracted, clearly.

Despite all my machinations, activism, and worldbuilding, my educational life was about to run parallel with my romantic life as a past-tense event. As I listened to Kyle, my attention was really focused on a letter I was twitching in between my fingers and thumb as Kyle spoke. It was on resume stock; the senders wanted to make sure I understood how serious the situation was. I had read the letter enough times to have it committed to memory. It was a serious blow to my life situation, this one more serious than any before. I was in a mess of my own making again, however accidental. But rather than re-read the letter again, I let my soon-to-be-ex-boyfriend vent as my mind flew elsewhere. At least the breakup was a distraction from the monotony of classes and the melodrama unfolding at school.

Although law school classes had been more or less the same for three years, my activities outside the classroom had taken on greater significance. CalSoc grew and grew, becoming more influential, and more than just a party machine. We shifted the school, throwing an anchor for future generations of students from California, bringing in more Californians, and creating programs that drove real change.

Nevertheless, none of those outside activities mattered to me anymore, except maybe as some sort of diversion. That was until I had stepped over an invisible line and was faced with the very real consequences of what happens when a student encroaches on what the administration saw as its territory. Sitting on the front stoop on that cold night being dumped by Kyle just didn't rate very high.

"I just don't get it," he said, clearly frustrated. He cared about me, and truthfully, I had been ignoring him. "It's like you don't even think to call me anymore."

"Listen, I'm sorry," I explained, too stoic to even shed a tear. "It wasn't your fault. I really do like you."

"You certainly don't act like it!" he stammered. "You literally just walk by me sometimes, like you don't even see me." He was not wrong.

"Oh," I muttered as a cold breeze caused me to pull my jacket in closer. "Yeah…I guess I've been distracted…and I forgot to tell you that I'm being expelled." I said it matter-of-factly, as if he should have known, but really, I had just dropped the academic equivalent on an atom bomb. I then showed him the letter I had been holding in my hand that whole time. I had not intentionally been hiding it, even for dramatic effect. I had just been so distracted by being expelled, I had forgotten to tell him or almost anyone else. My revelation landed with a predictable explosion.

He stood up, staring at me. "What?!" he yelled at me. "This is exactly what I'm talking about! How in the world could you not have told me that?" he screamed in exasperation.

My explanation was as calm as a court sentence; by then I had repeated the story enough times in my own head, and to a few defenders, I could recite it without emotion. I was not technically being expelled yet, though it certainly was on the docket. I was facing judicial proceedings that I had been told had a pre-ordained guilty verdict ending in expulsion. In my mind, I was being sent to a kangaroo court to teach me a lesson, and the school wanted to make sure I knew the end was a forgone conclusion. That was all there was to it.

Kyle, being the good-natured boyfriend he was, genuine to the core, was incensed. He, like the few other people I had told, was angry at how a law school founded, supposedly, on deep principles of ethics and justice could engage in such theatre and a mockery of its own stated ideals. Everyone had the same reaction, "You have to fight this, this is ridiculous, they can't do this, this is Columbia Law School, and they have to play by the rules, you didn't do anything wrong...." Believe me, I already knew that; I had heard it all before.

I stood to give Kyle a hug, and I told him not to worry; I would figure it out. But in the meantime, it was probably best we go our separate ways. Dating someone like me would not be good for his future. I cut the line and let him swim out to sea, while I struggled up four flights of stairs up to my apartment, going over the letter, and every event that led to it, again in my head.

An assistant dean for students had been sanguine about my prospects: "What did you expect?" she asked me privately one day.

"You know," I dryly joked. "For a school that says they want you to push the boundaries, they're really quite unimaginative."

Here's what happened. It had started with CalSoc, of course. The school was only too happy for me to create a happier environment it could market in competition for students with Harvard and Yale. The administration was willing to look the other way at my unorthodox but legal methods, as long as I could at least give the appearance of abiding by the letter of the law regarding student organizations. But, like Icarus, I flew too close to the sun. The initial sparks flew when CalSoc began programs that were considered duplicative of career programs run by the law school itself. Not surprisingly, the dean of career services seemed less than thrilled by that, and she threatened to send a letter to every law firm in town calling me a "rogue actor" and a host of other things that would endanger CalSoc fundraising and function. Rather than find a quiet resolution, I put all my chips on black, and I filed a formal complaint of harassment against her.

Although the dean who was the subject matter of my complaint left the school shortly after I filed it, I decided to publicize the matter by feeding information to a blogger, who ran with it. Then things really escalated.

First, I was taken to task by an assistant dean for students, though she could barely keep a straight face. Then came the dean of administration, followed by the dean of students.

Finally, the dean of the law school himself summoned me, unhappy to have to even speak to a student, much less negotiate with one. At this point, I was also wondering how many deans there possibly were, to which I still had no answer except perhaps one less than before my escapade.

Had the school done nothing, the whole thing would have gone away. This was, at first glance, a ridiculous fight over nothing. A single blog post about an administrator who had, in fact, threatened a student. In the relatively small law school world, these were damaging revelations but hardly long-term fodder for injury. Outside the insular world of Columbia, they barely registered. Had cooler heads prevailed, there would have been nothing to talk about. But this was the Ivy League, and cooler heads took a back seat to ego.

The school wanted an apology from me, or so it seemed, for publicizing my complaint. That I would not give. An acorn of righteousness had apparently been planted at DePauw and grown into a strong tree. My indignation was grounded not just on this fight with the dean of career services but on something much deeper. I had discovered information I felt revealed my alma mater to be disingenuous and, potentially, at odds with the very principles it purported to uphold. I had copies of sensitive and revealing data the school had accidentally posted, which I had found long ago on a drive accessible to students. This data, I believed, showed that the school decidedly did not live up to what it claimed to hold so dear. What those documents showed, to me, was that the school—for all its claims of rigor and righteousness—was actually just a perpetual motion machine in service of prestige and rankings.

To me, there might not have been a clearly demarcated bright red line in what was expected of law schools by the American Bar Association, but there was still a line, and Columbia Law had very concretely crossed it in my worldview.

Just consider the concept of grading. Testing appeared to be structured so that the vast majority of students would get a good grade. Take home exams were encouraged to keep grades high. Exam questions and answers were given in advance to keep grades high. High grades meant people got hired at top-tier law firms. This meant that Columbia Law's post-graduate employment rate stayed high. That meant its reputation for placing students at the best firms also stayed high. Employment placement and overall reputation were two of the most important factors in law school rankings, which dictated the school's elite status and fundraising success. That, in my opinion, ignored the entire purpose of law school: to teach students to be thoughtful and creative advocates. Institutionally speaking, Columbia Law School instead existed just to continue in greatness, in my opinion.

In the law school ecosystem, this should have been an earthquake. And for once, it would have mattered outside our little echo chamber on the Upper West Side. If a more than 200-year-old bastion of American education tumbles because its pursuit of greatness was premised on deeply flawed aims and methods, that's good click bait for any news outlet. The night I first found those files on a random storage drive, I realized the same thing I realized the first night I threw a party: everyone here was just like me, trying to be something they were not. They were just getting away with it.

In the process of my war with the school over an apology about publicizing my complaint against the dean of career services, I told an assistant dean I had this information. I suppose internally among the school administrators, there might have been a series of conversations along the following lines: what if this student went public again with what he uncovered? What reputational damage would it cause? I can only imagine the powers that be would prefer that I not only not have the evidence but that I not be around to use it.

Of course, I knew nothing of those conversations or even if they occurred. What I knew was the result: sitting on the stoop with my soon-to-be ex-boyfriend, facing an internal judicial hearing that, I suspected, wouldn't be much of a hearing at all.

My letter threatening expulsion, the one I memorized and held between my fingers as my boyfriend dumped me, had come just a few days after that conversation with the assistant dean. I was being placed under something that resembled a judicial review but which wasn't much of one at all. Instead of being subjected to a trial, as called for in the school's policies, a special single inquisitor was appointed. I would not be allowed to see the evidence against me, nor the specific wording of the charges and accusations. I was simply informed in one letter of the single charge against me, the violation of a "Rule 4.1.2," which did not actually exist, constituting a "violation of integrity." This was, it was clear to me, going to be just a Soviet-style show trial, along with the pre-ordained punishment.

I wasn't really shocked by what the whole thing was about, but I was shocked it was actually happening and that no one wanted to do anything about it. I had long since learned at DePauw that my fellow students would be of no help. Everyone's ready to protest some problem in a faraway land, but if you brought something close to home, you're nuclear.

But it was when an ethics professor I knew, whom I asked to testify on my behalf, bowed out of the process that I realized the jig was probably up, and things were more serious this time around.

"No, no, no," she bawled over the phone in a thick Long Island accent. "Just because I teach this stuff does not mean I can get involved. No, no, no. They're after you. I can't have them after me too." Slack-jawed, I hung up. It did not bode well for my case: the most principled legal ethics lawyer I knew had agreed with me but refused to speak up. A few outside lawyers were interested in the case in the abstract but not in taking on the House Targaryen of the legal world. Several bloggers were interested, but that really would be a major attack, and though I was inclined to pass along what I had found to them in a bold but ill-advised self-defensive maneuver, something inside still gave me pause.

I did really want it all to be fine. I had gone to Columbia to find myself, not to destroy others. I had certainly made some poor strategic decisions, if justified, and ethical ones, but my dreams had not changed.

That night, sitting on the stoop outside my front door, where Kyle had met me, I thought about giving him my whole story, from cookies to red boots, from one school and life crisis to another. "Maybe that's what this was all about, some fateful karmic push forward to embrace my own crackpot journey," I thought, "except this time I would win." As soon as the thought entered my mind, however, so did pictures of Kevin, Brady, and Mandy running away at DePauw; glimpses of a brick held over my head by Omid at USC; the sound of water trickling through the mountains in Idyllwild. How would he possibly understand all that, when even the very possibility of endangering his clerkship was enough to give him pause?

So instead, I had gone up to my apartment and wondered what the hell was coming next. Lying in bed, I checked my email one last time. There was one from a teacher at the law school I had grown to respect the most, Professor X. He was a high-flying, pre-eminent figure at Columbia. He was beloved by students and treasured by the administration. And now, as I stood at the precipice, higher than any before, he would be a completely unexpected parachute. The email read: "Come see me at ten a.m. tomorrow. Professor X." I was being summoned to his apartment. And it was not the type of call you turn down.

CHAPTER 16

THE CHOICE

Whenever I had visited Professor X's apartment, it had always been the same routine. He kept a professional distance, never too friendly or familiar. Everyone was Mr. Edwards or Ms. Smith, no matter their age. One always knew which students were closest because they were called by their first names. Visits were usually in the evening, and there was usually scotch or a gin martini floating around, but never meals. Like first names, food was for a select few. He was always "present" and focused on his guests, never stealing away for a call or an email. He was a welcome reminder of the gentility of a past era, and that appeal, combined with his innate politeness and kindness, made him the object of his students' devotion.

When I arrived the morning after his email, there was no scotch or gin. I was shown into his study, a room I had never actually seen him at work in. Yet there he was, surrounded by stacks of papers and books, like a professor in the movies. I had figured he was only the image of a professor, a font of elegance where words just sprouted from his mind into best-selling books, not a researcher or someone who toiled.

Professor X set aside his papers and lit a cigar. "A bad habit," he would often admit, "but one I can't quite seem to give up."

We sat there in silence for a few moments as the pepper-laced scent from the tobacco smoke remained, suspended in the air.

"Well, Mister Greiwe," he began with a sigh. "You seem to have gotten yourself into a great deal of trouble." His words also hung in the air like the smoke from his cigar. I had not reached out to him about my crisis, so word must have gotten to him somehow.

"Yes, well," I began to explain. His expression immediately shifted; it was clear he was not interested in explanations. I changed course but was unsure of where he wanted me to go. "I certainly am," I said, though I couldn't let go of at least one protestation. "But I haven't done anything wrong."

"The school," Professor X said, referring to the dean of the law school by his first name, "seems to feel differently. They really want to make an example of you."

None of this was news to the professor or me, so I wasn't sure what he was getting at. Professor X got up from behind his desk and invited me to walk with him around the apartment and eventually onto the balcony. He had one of those balconies that are rare in Manhattan; it ran the full length of his apartment, overlooking the city.

As we walked, he engaged in almost kind of monologue, punctuated only briefly by my saying, "Yes, sir," or "How so?" This man who had kept those around him at arm's length revealed personal feelings concerning me that I had not been aware he held.

"You see, Mister Greiwe, you are what my uncle used to call a 'Can-Do Man,'" he began, deploying a phrase he used regularly, as if he had just coined it. "You're someone who can be trusted, who can get things done, who can accomplish great things. And I truly believe that. You can do some really great things. I want you to help me do great things. You have a very bright future ahead of you…if you can stay focused. Not as a lawyer or professor or judge, but as someone who can do something bigger."

I stood still but nodded.

"But then there is this…matter…this little trouble you've gotten yourself into. Let me assure you that what may or may not have actually happened is not really the issue here. It's really quite something.

"You know, they, ah, called me to give me a heads up about this. They know, of course, I'm quite fond of you, and given how they feel about me, they felt the need to tell me, and you know, they honestly, truly want to get rid of you. It's quite the predicament."

He stared blankly at me. Almost as if I were supposed to say something, but I was without words. Thirty minutes had gone by, and I still had no idea what this conversation was about. Was this a eulogy? Was this a lament about lost potential? Was this a fond farewell? Was he in a predicament too? Professor X had given no real indications yet.

Then almost offhandedly, he let drop, "I told them, of course, that was not going to happen."

"I don't understand," I replied, still not getting what he was saying.

"Of course, something must happen," he went on, as if he had not heard me, or as if I should have understood. He continued at a measured pace, matter-of-factly, with the assuredness that comes from being accustomed to being listened to.

"There will be in inquiry, and you'll let it play out, but it will be nothing to worry about. They'll get to say they did their part holding you accountable, but you'll face no consequence. It will be as if the matter never happened."

"Which means…what exactly?" I asked. I knew something was coming, but I *still* didn't know what.

"They'll wait until the last day of next semester, and on graduation, they'll free you. We can put this whole mess behind us, behind *you*, Mister Greiwe."

There it was, here today and gone tomorrow, with the wave of some magical administrative wand. Much taken aback by this once again idiosyncratic form of salvation, I stood there, silent.

"Mister Greiwe, this is a good offer," he said, sensing my reluctance.

As Professor X stared over the weathered brick parapet of the balcony, out across the city with his cigar, he let his words resonate in my mind. Fantastical visions of some switch simply being flicked ran in my head. I could blow it all up instead of taking this offer. It was one of those moments where one had multiple fantasies about what one could do. Like walking into a crowded elevator and wailing at the top of your lungs or showing up to the office naked, things that never come to pass but that are cathartic daydreams.

If I pushed the button, if I came forward with every document I had, I would show the world and let them determine if Columbia was living up to its own standard. I'd stand on principle, and I'd *show them*.

For once, I was not powerless. For once, I had leverage; for once, I had something that felt like control, even if it was self-destructive, mean, and vicious. I had a sense of righteous indignation, something that doesn't cost a poor kid a dime. My professors at DePauw may have cultivated my feelings of loss for their own purposes, but now this feeling was my own. In that moment on the balcony, I didn't share my fantasy, but my frustration exploded onto the good, peace-brokering Professor.

I stood for a moment pulling myself together. "I didn't do anything wrong. I'm being put on trial. Actually, I'm not *even* getting a trial, it's some sort of pre-ordained decision for breaking a rule that doesn't even exist, and one I didn't break even if it did exist," I said for what seemed like the millionth time. Even then I knew my protest was a last gasp of defiance, not a response to what he was saying.

All the drama, the anxiety, fear, and intense pressure had cost me many sleepless nights, lost friends, had made me question everything I thought I knew. This life-shattering tsunami was all going to go away in a puff of cigar smoke. Seemed a bit farfetched, but I was pretty sure that's what was going on. Anti-climactic does not even begin to describe the absurd situation I found myself in. Yet here I was. I knew I was going to go along and that it was the right thing to do in the long run.

"Mister Greiwe," he sighed. He waited a few moments. "You have a choice. Make the right one. This problem, this thing, it's all not worth it. You are capable of doing so much more, but you will never do it, if you spend all your time allowing your feet to get caught up in these weeds. Move on to something bigger and better."

I stood there for a few moments, the wind whipping around us. I nodded to him silently and left with a firm handshake and a forced smile. I can't even remember if I actually thanked him out loud or not, though I would in the coming months. I was in trouble and alone; even my newfound family could not have helped me with this one. But without anyone asking, this man had simply stepped up and imposed a solution with the authority of Solomon.

Per his offer, I went through the kangaroo court, as it appeared to me. But it was even more comical than I expected. I heard nothing for weeks as the semester dragged on until they called me into the inquisitor's office. I had a single interview that lasted fewer than ten minutes where, in a surprising twist, she asked me if I was sorry. That was what they had wanted to hear: me tell everyone I was sorry. After all this, that's still all they wanted. Yet I wasn't sure what I was being asked to even apologize for.

I sat there, confused. All this, all these months of anxiety, stress, and isolation, it had been mental torture. The hoops I had to jump through. In the end, it simply came down to a woman sitting across a desk, asking me if I was sorry? An act of theatre, a ridiculous power trip, a symbolic power play by the administration?

I had gone to Columbia in hopes of finding myself. I had achieved social success, true, but the rest was all just a bad replay of my undergraduate career. I was not any better off professionally as far as I could see, graduating from law school with honors but no intention of being a lawyer and no back-up plan. Now, here I found myself sitting across from a woman asking me for an apology, and none of that mattered. The last three years were supposed to move me forward, not leave me as adrift as in Los Angeles. In this moment, it seemed I had done nothing and gained nothing.

"I'm sorry that all of this happened," I replied, truly sincere for the first time in months. I was sorry I had gone to Columbia Law. I was sorry I had been caught up in my own little world of CalSoc, meaningless beyond these walls. I was sorry for the relationships I had lost. Most of all, I was sorry I had not learned from the lessons of the past. I vowed silently I would not make the same mistake again but all the same knowing I probably would until I found some way to end the cycle.

I had come here with ambition and what I thought was a plan. I had spent my life in Indiana chasing normal. In LA, I had thought I could find it. In New York, I believed I would create one on my own. This place would be *the* place... building on the foundation of my new family, embracing the excitement of first love, and finding a path to a stable future and career, whatever that might be. It turned out to be none of what I wanted or anticipated.

Maybe life does not like it when you make plans or when you try to dictate the terms of engagement. As I left the inquisitor's office with a summary dismissal, both of us knowing what my future would be, I felt a deep sense of emptiness, combined with the first real understanding of who I was. I had spent so much time trying to build up the outside of a person that I had been taken by surprise to discover what it meant to be someone on the inside, however small this new feeling was.

I found myself short of breath, my face flush with embarrassment as a crushing sense of the reality set in. I raced through the hallways of Jerome Greene Hall, pushing my way into the elevator. Mercifully, I was by myself for the quick trip down to the ground floor. That familiar "ding," and in twenty paces, I was out into the middle of a tree-filled, leafless courtyard.

I ran to the wall, panting. There I was, feeling as naked as the trees around me. I had tasted the bitter fruit of the Tree of Self Knowledge and could not avoid the consequences. I was overcome with embarrassment, feeling totally exposed and left only with a handful of painful memories and destabilizing realizations. All my insane experiences trying to be someone else had in fact *created a person*, just not one I wanted to be or know until this moment. Chasing normal had turned me into someone very normal after all. Normal, though, just turned out to be a very messed up place, a toxic by-product of experiences you don't plan for or learn from in the right way.

Little pieces came into focus. It turns out I was often an absentee boyfriend. I was principled in conflict but willing to compromise, even if it meant violating those principles to win. I was eager to please those around me, but out of a sense of utility and purpose, not joy or comfort. I was alone, even though I had a family and a friend. I was sad and embarrassed to have felt like I wasted over twenty years of my life.

My litany of revelations would stay with me, while the five elements of a tort, and the interpretation of felony murder, and the sense of entitlement from Columbia Law disappeared or blended into my past as one long blur of a very odd life. I had discovered these lessons during my three years in law school, but it was all to what end? While others were set to go to on to well-paid jobs or clerkships, I was standing in an empty plaza, really no better off than that first week when I sat in the front row with my pink fluffy pen. I had come to find myself. What I found was crushing and unflattering. Something told me maybe I should have made better use of my time; on the other hand, the lessons I learned in New York changed my life and may not have been learned any other way. I had been chasing normal and discovered what that meant in my world, if still not yet how to live it.

CHAPTER 17

BREAKING THE CYCLE
AT A ROUND TABLE

Graduation was a blur. I was the chair of my class at Columbia Law, but in a break from tradition, I was prohibited from speaking out of concern over what I might say during the ceremony. I walked down the aisle and sat onstage next to the very dean who attempted to run me out of school and blankly stared ahead for hours in the unrelenting sunshine. I listened to the man I selected to be our graduation speaker. I watched classmates whose social lives I helped build. I received my honor cords and degree and a letter that said I had been found guilty of some undefined charges. The only punishment I would receive, it said, was the destruction of any records associated with my inquiry. Even the man responsible for ensuring my presence on that stage, Professor X, had not bothered to attend.

As the sun beat down on me, I knew it was time to leave New York and go back to Los Angeles. There was nothing left for me in Manhattan, and I was now armed with a family and a friend in Kate, as well as the knowledge I had been becoming someone all along, even though I hadn't known it and didn't like him very much. It was now incumbent on me to stop running away and instead try and build a "home," something I had never had before. For someone who had been running since the age of nine, chasing that ever-elusive normal, it all felt very strange. Getting advice from Miss A. at the Idyllwild Strawberry Creek Inn was one thing, but putting it into practice was something very different.

Dinner that night, however, felt familiar, if only because of who was there. I was surrounded by people, for the first time, who loved and supported me. Lori, Kate, my parents, and siblings all flew in to celebrate this milestone. None of them knew how I'd made it to graduation, and it never even occurred to them I might not view this ending as anything to celebrate or that I had never even known what a celebration like this was before. I had heard of other people having special parties for events in their lives, but I was never the beneficiary of such celebrations. Hell, most of my life, I did not even make note of my own birthday.

As we gathered at a large round table, I could almost see the epilogue of my past and script for my future being laid out at Brasserie 8½. In the famous dining rooms of New York, the lives of the rich and famous were played out in public, politicians mingled with mafiosos, and relationships were born and ended. That night in May 2009, one of those restaurants, a flight below street level in Midtown, hosted the end of one of many stages of the exhausting, and ultimately, fruit-less, chase of my youth. The people seated next to me were almost perfectly cast for the purpose.

The future was not yet written, but I knew it would include these people. That's the lesson I needed to learn: life was not about chasing or defining what normal was. Rather, it was about learning to live life itself. And I had finally started living it, and would continue to live it, with the people who surrounded me on this summer night for a graduation dinner, these people who loved *me* for the messed-up person *I* was. No realization could have been more heartwarming or filled me more with relief, after having spent the better part of two decades trying to be like other people. That night, my present and my future were right in front of me as I gazed around the table at each person.

Lori was seated across from me with her red hair and huge personality. She was kind and generous, bubbly and gregarious, and could hold her own with anyone, including my siblings to either side of her. She loved me and had since Andrew Russ left me a shell of myself. She was emotive and needed someone to need her. Now that I had parents and was growing up, our relationship faded with time, as she became involved with others who offered her more. I looked up from my soup. She smiled, and I could see the sense of loss in her face, as I'm sure she saw in mine. She had previously been my savior, but now she was also a reminder of everything behind me. The collapse. My travails at Columbia, which she had been powerless to alleviate. She was the part of my past that I still wanted to have in my future.

To my left, that graduation night, was my mother, who applauded everyone and everything that could possibly involve me and our family. She had woven me into her life and memories as if I had always been there. She was relishing this achievement of mine, as her son, and she made a point of it. She was the type of woman who didn't have specific preferences often, but when she did, she always got her way. She was the one who insisted I take the bar exam even though I did not want to be a lawyer; it would be useful, she said. She was the one who lent an empathetic ear in every breakup to come, even though she saw them coming before I did. In the following years, I grew into her embrace, something I still do not fully understand but that I've grown used to accepting. It feels like what I imagine babies feel when their mothers hug them for the first time.

I heard that next year, she and my father were back at a Christmas party in their previous neighborhood. My mother bragged to an old friend about her son's graduation from law school, to which her friend answered, "I didn't know Robbie went to law school," referring to my brother.

My mother simply said, "No, he didn't. It's my other son." The woman looked confused.

"I lived next to you for fifteen years," she replied. "You only have one son."

"No, I have two," my mom said in a chipper, upbeat voice, not even acknowledging the change in reality. She did not even bother to explain the details; she just went for another glass of wine. Life was what she made it; others could get on the train or not. I would eventually find her confidence a shelter in future storms. And she would ensure her love and affection were always a safe harbor.

My siblings were scattered around the table. Kelley, the oldest, would date and break up with my law school roommate, against my advice. But like my mother, I was a family member for her, and it was good to see her. Kristen, the youngest, took longer to acclimate to my presence. We hadn't spoken much around the time I graduated, but when she realized I wasn't temporary, like a switch turning on, I became her brother. We would grow closer over the years, and I'd imagine our kids playing together in the way I never had before. Robbie, the one who had brought me into the family, would someday crack a joke about taking me out of it, and my mother's reprimand would mean our relationship would never be the same. He struggled to find his own path, but that graduation night, he was his better self and joined us all for a dinner filled with joy and reminiscence like I had never known.

To my right, Kate was involved in deep conversation with my father. Our Sundays had evolved, and we had become enmeshed deeper into each other's lives every week. She was the picture of elegance that evening, a glass of champagne in her long, thin hand. With the Chanel pearls from her boyfriend hanging from her neck, she glittered as a hostess should. She wanted this moment to be about me. She felt I deserved it, just as she insisted on throwing me a "going away" party a few weeks later. I swore no one would show up, but she made sure the club was full. Law school may have felt like a wash, but building my relationship with her was the first long-lasting, close friendship of my life. I would officiate at her wedding; I would later count her husband as close a friend as her. I would spend summer vacations in the Hamptons with them and go horseback riding in the English countryside.

Nine years later, I would lose her, like I had so many others in my life, but the very fact our friendship had existed would get me through it. I survived the loss because we had our love. We had grown as close as two humans could be: she called me one of her only three "soulmates" (the others being her husband and mother). There was nothing we did not share, until we didn't. Over a period, she'd grow more distant, to the point where we moved on with a clean but painful break. But as the light reflected off her glass that night under the chandelier of the restaurant, I didn't see this future. I saw only a driven hostess who would be the first and most honest definition of a "best friend" I would ever know.

Then, finally, there was my father. Rob was a man of few words; to this day, I can only guess he must have been complicit in, or at least casually accepting of, my adoption when it happened. That night, he smiled with pride for a young man he cared about; I didn't know if he thought of himself as my father then, but I certainly wanted him to.

A few years later, he would leave me speechless when I had decided to buy a house just a few blocks from where he and my mother lived. They were insistent, lovingly overbearing at times, that I purchase a home. It was part of the unsolicited parental advice they doled out increasingly often as the years went by, and it would take me a little while to see it for what it was: care.

We finally found a place, but it was well outside my budget range. They would not hear of letting it go, however, because of its proximity to their house, the investment value, and what it signified in my growth. In the grandest gesture of generosity, they gave me the down payment. I would still need to find a way to pay the mortgage...heavens the stress *that* would cause. But this generosity was unheard of for a poor kid from the sticks and indeed for most kids from anywhere. As my mother cheerfully set off to fetch wine, my father looked on as I sat there stunned.

"Are you okay?" he asked.

"I just don't know what to say," I replied. "I literally...it's too much. I can't even imagine...."

He shook his head, smiling. "This is what we do for our family. We're happy you're happy. We want to do this."

It was the first time he would ever call me family in front of me. That night over ten years before at Brasserie 8½, you could almost see the warmth in his smile, and his goodbye hug at the end of dinner felt like it would lead to every incredible moment that lay ahead.

Dinner went on with toast after toast, cheers to a sunny future that didn't acknowledge the pain of my past. I had spent so many years desperately holding onto those feelings and experiences, but these people were insisting I move on, if only by refusing to admit I could do anything but. We closed down the restaurant with faces beaming from wine and too many desserts. After we all trapsed out the front door, tipsy with alcohol and good feeling, with hugs all around, everyone bid farewell.

It was silent as I walked alone down the street to the sub-way. I had always liked New York in the spring before it was covered by the humid blanket of summer. It was as if the city were coming alive all over again. I was ready for a future that truly felt unwritten and filled with the prospects of untinged joy. That night, if I squinted hard enough at my past, I could see my own version of that magic. It was not what other people had, but now I knew that was the point. My life was mine, and it was time to start building my own, not modeling or borrowing from others.

I had spent the evening in the simplest of ways: a dinner with my family, a best friend, and a caring longtime mentor. Yet the very simplicity of that act was completely new and foreign to me. My story was crazy. Unique. Complicated. It was the culmination of years of running away, heartbreak, tur-moil, and abandonment. It was the result of an earnest search for stability and affection and years of repeated attempts to be of value to others. This turned out to be the dinner at the end of my ill-fated and ill-advised quest for normalcy.

My entire life, all I had wanted was to be normal. Yet all I might have needed was someone to tell me to stop trying. The people at dinner represented different signposts along the path of my life, each marked what it meant to discard the notion that others could define who I was or that I could even try to do so myself.

Normal was not something you got to dictate. Life was not something you mapped; it was something you lived. Of course, you could choose to go to law school; you could choose to break up with a boyfriend; you could choose to be a publicist, but each of those seemingly small choices became landmarks along a road filled with others' choices and a million little external factors you could drive yourself mad trying to prepare for, which I had tried, and failed, to do.

That night was eighteen years after I ran away from the original parents with my plate of cookies in search of the life I had seen on television and read about in books. A decade after trying to be like Kevin or be who my fraternity brothers wanted. A few hours after just barely escaping the law school train wreck I had accidentally engineered. I was finally starting my life. Running away had not been an opportunity to be like others. It was avoiding becoming myself. My choices, my crushing defeats, my near victories were the lead-up to learning life is full of heartbreak, joy, confusion, love, and loss for everyone. Mine would be different than everyone else's, but it would be no less real and no more typical.

That night, it felt like I was six inches off the ground as I walked down the pavement of West 57th street. I had stopped chasing something I thought I needed and learned to focus on what I had. I was finally moving forward authentically after trying so many times over the years. After time, I would come to realize the things you have, even when they're not what you planned, or wanted, or deserved, are who you are and what you need. I would one day learn accepting your life is the first step to making it better. There would be other lessons, just as tough, but that graduation night was a turning point, one that left me preoccupied with the massive revelation that life could be lived, and that was enough to start doing so.

My life is filled with so many examples of me chasing someone else's idea of normal, but I realized normal does not mean being the same as others. Rather, normal is being able to be whatever your true self is, without fear and with pride, both inside and out. If you are lucky enough to share life with people around you, say a prayer of gratitude for every moment.

For me, those prayers are filled with thankfulness, understanding, acceptance, and appreciation for the love, for the hurt, for the impact of Mrs. Cash, James, Andrew, Lori, Kevin, Brady, Professor X, and my family. In fact, anyone who gave me guidance, even people like Dale, Joan, Joe, and the endless Columbia deans. Good or bad, their actions and words led me to me who I became. As I jumped down the stairs to the subway home, I smiled at the thought. It was the first genuine smile I expressed to myself in years, if ever.

A NEW CHRISTMAS

A decade after that night at Brassiere 8½, I woke as I always do, gazing at the famous Hollywood sign out my bedroom window. I stood there, staring at the huge white letters on the hillside on a surprisingly clear day for LA. The view of that sign never gets old, and I feel incredibly fortunate that it's the first thing I get to see every morning. It might be too cliché, but cliches are born of truth. And the truth is, growing up the way I did, owning my own home, and with one of the most iconic views in the world, in a city like Los Angeles where dreams are made, seems as far-fetched as some rags to riches movie, as to be nearly unbelievable. But that is my story, one that, with all the drama, trauma, and then almost unbelievable joy, might sound like fiction but isn't.

This particular morning was no ordinary morning. It was the first Saturday in December, when I always host my holiday party. I love sitting around a cozy fire with a few friends and a good bottle of wine as much as anyone, but my holiday party was not that type of gathering. Over the years, it had unexpectedly grown into a black-tie *event*. For me, it was a celebration of everything I never imagined I would really have: hundreds of guests, friends, clients, and colleagues; a wonderful array of foods from spiced curry couscous to mini-shepherd's pies; real snow covering the lawn; and, as always, an unannounced special performance.

Later that night, as I went to announce the surprise centerpiece to the evening's festivities, I weaved my way through the throng, even wondering how so many people could fit in my house. I nevertheless hopped up on the stage in the yard to welcome everyone. I gestured, as I always do, toward my parents, telling them of my eternal gratitude, and then spoke to the assembled group with what felt like trite words about the holidays, the party, and what it meant to be surrounded by so many friends.

At that moment, time seemed to stop, with all my guests frozen in suspended animation. I looked out at the crowd; my gaze moved from face to face. There were almost two hundred people there. Sure, everyone likes the alcohol, food, and music of a good party, but this was *my* party, for *me*, yet they all showed up. Even as it was happening, I somehow doubted the reality of it all.

My mom and dad were leaning against a beam, holding each other. They loved me, and a decade later, I still struggled to really internalize that. Next to them was my roommate Jenny with her new fiancé. There had been many nights where Jenny sat with me on our steps, comforting me as I wondered aloud what I was even doing in the world in the first place. It didn't matter that I owned a house, had nice things, had close friends, and had built a successful career; I often still felt profoundly empty. I came to learn that, with the sort of childhood experiences I had endured, there's really no such thing as moving on, just moving forward without your past holding you back. That's…well, truly remarkable when you think about it, when all of the bad and all the good have both become part of who you are. You can only work toward making each day somehow better than the last, and that can make any day a pretty damn good one.

Back at my party, over in the corner of the room, was my kickball team. A kickball team! Me, in sports, with friends. I'm sure it would make the tortuous Coach K's head explode. As per instruction, they were all dressed to the nines. "Whoop, whoop, Craig!" one of them shouted, almost breaking my trance. Near them was a celebrity client whose next movie was about to come out, and next to him were the senior leaders of the firm I had just joined as an executive.

I continued to speak for few more moments. I was talking and apparently saying things that elicited laughter at the right moment, along with an emotional "aww!" when called for, but at the same time, it was an almost out-of-body experience. It felt like I was looking at this crowd of people, who were staring at me, but through someone else's eyes. So many people, so many relationships, so much effort. And almost none of them knew my whole story.

Yes, some of them knew bits and pieces generally. Being abandoned and adopted by Rob and Kathy was the headline most people knew, even if they lacked all of the gory details.

Growing up poor was not necessarily an uncommon reality, but I don't think a single person listening that night had ever had to experience hunger pains. But the rest of it? The words in these pages? Most likely, really foreign territory. Suddenly, I was struck by an overwhelming sense of distance. I finished my comments with a flourish and introduced the gospel choir I had engaged, who were sure to bring down the house.

As the singers took the stage to cheers and applause, I slipped out of the back yard and quietly made my way into the house and upstairs. Like in my fraternity days, the upstairs of the house was closed off, and I found solace and refuge in my bedroom, closing the white wooden door behind me.

I stood there, looking at the Hollywood sign, barely visible at night (I always wonder why it's not lit up, what a shame), and it was like I was a reflection of my earlier self that morning. I set down my drink, tequila soda having years ago replaced the vodka cranberries of my youth, and stood there silently with my eyes closed. I felt the velvet lapel of my tuxedo, the pull of the button of the jacket, the tightness of my new shoes, not yet "broken in." As a kid who never had shoes, I relished having dozens of pairs, and this particular pair had looked so great in the store window I had impulsively bought them in spite of myself. A pair of black dress shoes for $300! "Crazy, crazy!" I thought to myself then. Yet, I handed over the credit card, making a purchase I could never have thought to afford in my youth. So different from my cookies all those years before, but I have learned some things do come full circle in unexpected ways.

I could hear the rumbling of the music and voices through the windows. Just on the other side of the wall, there were hundreds of people listening to Christmas songs being sung across octaves at my own house at my own party, with my own friends, complete with my own caterer, a very long way from staring at barely edible, cheap Po' boys (I could never have imagined!). But there I was, in that moment, still feeling alone in the darkness, staring in the opposite direction. It felt disconcertingly familiar. How had this moment ever come to pass?

It wasn't that I was running away from something terrible, I thought to myself. That much had changed. So why was I in my room alone? What had driven me away from a party full of happy people and love? As I opened my eyes, it came to me exactly why. Just like the day so many years earlier when I first arrived in California, as I stood on stage that night, I felt a tightening in my chest. I saw all those people waiting for me to say something, and I realized that none of them really knew my whole story, and that was the problem. Right there, in plain view of everyone, I was having an anxiety attack. The difference between then and now was that I was physically and emotionally strong enough to hold myself together, long enough to finish my remarks and high-tail it up to my room for a momentary respite.

Now here I was, decades later, a changed man, succumbing to an anxiety attack on a night that should be filled with celebration. The pain didn't take away from any of the joy I had experienced at earlier parties or the joy of that night. It had nothing to do with the joy, in fact. It was simply a reminder that we all each carry our own stories and our own pain with us. It doesn't have to weaken us; it can make us stronger. I know what I've been through. While I'll always be fearful of losing it all, no matter how far I go, I also know what I've done…. I could do it again. A poor kid will always be fearful of having no money no matter how well they do. I am. I'm an abused kid who will likely always wonder if someone truly loves them (I sometimes do), but people can grow beyond those feelings without erasing or forgetting their past.

I had set out from the very beginning chasing normal. After years of failing in that pursuit, I had become a person I didn't like. But thankfully, in the process, I realized that "normal" is simply living the most rewarding life you can create for yourself and, just as importantly, for those you love. In my case, it was after law school that I began living the life of the person I wanted to be, making choices that defined me on my own, not as a reflection of others. I was imperfect. I made a lot more mistakes. I suffered from depression for many more years before finding a way out of the darkness. And yes, I had an anxiety attack at a party I was throwing, even though the moment was filled with love. Life is messy. Life will always be messy. It's what you make of that mess that matters.

As I stood there, staring out in the distance pondering this personal revelation, I smiled to myself. Now I could smile through it all genuinely and compassionately. I heard the gospel choir wrapping up their set. The soloist hit a high note, and it filled me with joy. I heard someone bounding up the stairs.

"Craig!" I heard my mother call. The upstairs was off limits to guests, but my mother was never a guest. Noticing my absence from the party, she was looking for me. I remembered how many things had thankfully changed in twenty years. She knocked gently on the door and opened it.

"Craig?"

I turned around, my tears now dry.

"Hi," I said, smiling.

"What are you doing up here?" She asked.

"I'm just trying to take it all in," I said, warmly smiling back at her. "It's a lot sometimes."

"That's a good thing," she said firmly.

I nodded, standing for a moment before moving toward her. I gave her a hug, the kind of embrace filled with love that I had desperately wanted for so long and now wonderfully got to feel many times over.

"Come on," I said after we finished hugging. "Let's go back down to the party."

We went back downstairs, I took a deep breath, and I dove back into my life, still filled with all the contradiction I had in my head but also filled with more real things and real relationships of value than I ever could have imagined. When I stopped Chasing Normal, then and only then, did I find a life I wanted to live.

ACKNOWLEDGMENTS

This book is the story of my childhood and the years that followed, though I had tried as hard as possible to forget them. It's all true, though perhaps my memories are imperfect, as they should be. It's all my opinion, anyway.

As with any memoir, there were difficult choices to make in telling my story. This is just one true thread of many that became my life. There are wonderful people who played key roles in my life who do not appear. There are evil people who played key roles in my life who also do not appear. This is just one collection of stories, as best I can remember, with some literary license here and there. For nearly everyone in it, reading this book will be the first they hear of its existence.

I am grateful both to those who positively inspired me and those who provided the honest, incredible fodder for the ridiculous, wild, and crazy life I have lived. It all came together in these pages.

And finally, thank you to Jeff Schmidt, the agent who landed me my first ISBN, JWR for your thoughtful guidance, and Post Hill Press, the publisher willing to take a shot on a poor kid from the sticks who became somebody with a story to tell after all. Let's do something great in this world together, something that inspires joy.

ABOUT THE AUTHOR

Craig Greiwe is a business executive and former Chief Strategy Officer for one of America's largest culture and marketing firms, as well as a former Los Angeles mayoral candidate—but it wasn't always that way. He grew up in poverty in rural Indiana, before being abandoned as a teenager. He worked hard, relied on the blessings of others, and built a life from virtually nothing. Now, he's known for finding solutions to seemingly impossible problems and developing groundbreaking strategy for America's most trusted businesses, all while making sure that every friend has a drink in their hand, a warm shoulder to cry on, and a "chin-up" perspective. He has a relentlessly optimistic yet practical outlook on life—the kind you can only develop by having hit rock bottom and dusting yourself off to try again.